word alive

In-depth Small Group Bible Studies

STUDY GUIDE

Ephesians

MW01678784

EPHESIANS

more than we ask or imagine

Dale Cooper

FAITH ALIVE Christian Resources

Grand Rapids, Michigan

Unless otherwise noted, Scripture quotations in this publication are from the HOLY BIBLE, NEW INTERNATIONAL VERSION, © 1973, 1978, 1984, International Bible Society. Used by permission of Zondervan Bible Publishers.

Cover photo: Jupiter Images

Word Alive: In-depth Small Group Bible Studies

Note: This study material is revised from the Revelation Series format in which it was first published in 1996. "Additional Notes" sections in this study guide were written by Kenneth A. Baker, author of the leader's guide for this study.

We welcome your comments. Call us at 1-800-333-8300 or e-mail us at editors@faithaliveresources.org.

www.FaithAliveResources.org

ISBN 978-1-59255-284-9

10 9 8 7 6 5 4 3 2

Contents

Introduction

From halfway across the Roman Empire, the apostle Paul writes to his beleaguered Christian friends in Ephesus, urging them "to keep the unity of the Spirit" so that they can "live a life of love" in Christ (Eph. 4:3; 5:2). Though Paul himself is in prison, he encourages these believers with praise upon praise about who God is and what this great God has done for them.

With immeasurable love God has chosen these believers from eternity in Christ to be his adopted children (1:4-5). And Christ, who now sits at the right hand of God "far above all rule and authority" (1:21), has redeemed them "through his blood" (1:7)—both Jews and Gentiles—making them "God's people and members of God's household" (2:19). In this way believers begin to enjoy "the riches of [God's] glorious inheritance" even now (1:18). What's more, God strengthens his children continually "with power through his Spirit" so that Christ may live in their hearts "through faith" (3:16-17). And by that power they can "grasp" and experience the vast love of this God, "who is able to do immeasurably more than all we ask or imagine" (3:18-20).

In God's "incomparably great power" (1:19) in Christ, all believers can "live a life worthy of the calling [they] have received" (4:1): to be the church, the body of Christ (1:22-23), making salvation known throughout the universe (3:10). Together we who believe can unite in the Spirit, using the gifts God gives us to build each other up toward maturity (4:3, 12-13, 16) and to submit to one another in love, following Christ's example (5:1-2, 21). In the power of the Holy Spirit we can even fend off the attacks of the devil (6:11). Equipped with "the armor of God" and praying "in the Spirit on all occasions," we can "stand firm" (6:11, 14, 18)—"to the praise of [God's] glory" (1:14).

—Paul Faber, for Faith Alive Christian Resources

Dale Cooper, author of this study guide, served for many years as chaplain at Calvin College, Grand Rapids, Michigan. Kenneth A. Baker, author of the accompanying leader's guide, is a Christian Reformed pastor in Kalamazoo, Michigan.

Cool refreshment for parched heads and hearts.

1

EPHESIANS 1:1-10

From Eternity, for All Things, Forever

Ephesians 1:1-10

1Paul, an apostle of Christ Jesus by the
will of God,

To the saints in Ephesus, the faithful in
Christ Jesus:

2Grace and peace to you from God our
Father and the Lord Jesus Christ.

3Praise be to the God and Father of our
Lord Jesus Christ, who has blessed us in
the heavenly realms with every spiritual
blessing in Christ. 4For he chose us in him
before the creation of the world to be holy
and blameless in his sight. In love 5he
predestined us to be adopted as his sons
through Jesus Christ, in accordance with
his pleasure and will—6to the praise of his
glorious grace, which he has freely given us
in the One he loves. 7In him we have
redemption through his blood, the forgive-
ness of sins, in accordance with the riches of
God's grace 8that he lavished on us with all
wisdom and understanding. 9And he
made known to us the mystery of his will
according to his good pleasure, which he
purposed in Christ, 10to be put into effect
when the times will have reached their
fulfillment—to bring all things in heaven
and on earth together under one head,
even Christ.

"Can I *Really* Be Sure Jesus Loves Me?"

Pope Gregory I, who served as a spiritual leader to Christians throughout the Western world from A.D. 590-604, received a letter one day from an elderly, faithful Christian woman. She was troubled about her sins and wondered if she could be sure that Jesus loved her.

The woman asked the church leader, simply and directly, "Can I know, beyond doubt, that Jesus is my Savior and that he will love me forever?" The pope's response: "Yes, for sure." Then she wrote another letter, asking, "How?" The response: "You must believe that he is your Savior from your sins, *and* you must do good and righteous things to show that you love him." In a third letter the woman asked, "What kinds of things? And how many?" The pope replied, "You can do a whole variety of things to show Jesus your love. You can pray, give to the poor, show mercy, worship, be kind . . . lots of things. And how many? Well, you can always do more, of course. . . ." In her final letter the woman asked again, "Holy Father, if I can—and must—always do more, then can I *really* be sure Jesus loves me?" The pope's answer: "You can be *almost* sure."

These searching questions and uncertain answers from 1,400 years ago place us squarely in the midst of vexing issues that affect us still today. And that gives us a fine place to begin our study of Ephesians, because this letter of Paul, soaked richly in spiritual insight and direction, addresses doubts and uncertainty we can have at any age and in any era.

Every chapter of Ephesians is cool refreshment for parched heads and hearts, nourishment for hungering souls. Continually in this letter Paul talks of "the riches of God's grace" (Eph. 1:7) provided for us "in Christ." Paul encourages his readers—including us—to receive these riches so that "we will in all things grow up into him who is the Head, that is Christ" (4:15) and "be filled to the measure of all the fullness of God" (3:19).

In for a Treat

Ephesians is chock-full of key words marking the contours of the gospel message. Paul refers to "glory" four times; "grace" eleven times; "fullness," "fills," and "filled" six times; and—the font of all these riches—"in Christ" fourteen times. Studying these chapters, savoring these immense truths, we're in for a treat. My prayer—and, I trust, yours too—is that God's Spirit will use what we do together to bring each of us closer to "unity in the faith and in the knowledge of the Son of God . . . attaining to the whole measure of the fullness of Christ" (4:13). In the first several lessons (on Eph. 1-3) we'll focus with Paul on what God has done for us in Christ; then we'll examine Paul's instructions on what these teachings mean for living the Christian life together as God's people.

"An Apostle . . . to the Saints"

Few things in life are more exciting—and few positions more privileged and honored—than to be the first to announce an important piece of good news.

God is actively pursuing a grand, vital work in this broken, tired world. The divine rescue effort from trouble, sorrow, discord, and death is as wide and deep and high and long as the reach of the entire universe. What's more, this work is infinitely more pervasive than the sin that damages good things in God's creation. God's goal is no less than that of bringing "all things in heaven and on earth together under one head, even Christ" (1:10). And Paul, by the will of this very God, has the privilege of announcing this good news. Paul is an "apostle," a person sent on a mission.

When Paul wrote this letter of Ephesians, he was in prison in Rome (3:1; 4:1; 6:20)—probably around A.D. 60—waiting to appear before Caesar for being a missionary for Christ (see Acts 21:27-26:32; 28:11-31). But by no means did Paul consider himself a victim of unfortunate circumstances. As we can see from his buoyant mood and confident outlook, Paul knew that in a way far deeper and more penetrating than what appeared on the surface of events, God was at work at the very heart of history, and Paul, as herald, was participating in God's mission to the world.

Paul begins his letter by wishing his readers "grace and peace" amid the troubling circumstances they faced as new believers in Christ. Though it was a common enough greeting in those days, "grace and peace" for Paul was no meaningless formality. "Grace" (*charis*), one of the richest words in the New Testament, identifies closely with "joy" (*chara*). Grace is "the spring and source of joy," and Paul uses it as shorthand to denote all the riches supplied by God in Christ. "Peace," a word recalling the deeply profound Hebrew sense of *shalom,* reminds Paul's readers of the delightful "singing together" of all creation, as God originally intended it. Where God's creation flourishes in justice and righteousness, *shalom* is at work. By wishing his readers "grace and peace," Paul shows that he longs for his friends to enjoy the very best in life, the deep, lasting joy and peace that are possible only through God in Christ. As "saints," after all, these friends—like Paul—are holy people set apart by God to become more and more like Jesus.

Chosen in Christ for God's Glory

In verse 3 Paul begins a torrent of words that runs on for eleven verses—all in one sentence in the original Greek text. But only grammarians protest. Paul is being swept away with delirious joy as he tries to describe all the wonders God has done for his people through Jesus Christ.

Paul stretches back before time and into eternity to say that, yes, even before time began, God was thinking about his people, loving them, and planning their deliverance and new life in Christ. Of course, what Paul is teaching here extends far beyond our own capacities to embrace. But to him two facts are clear: (1) his own sad, sinful past is proof that we are all dead in our sins; and (2) our salvation is not hastily thought up as some stopgap measure to counteract human sin. From eternity itself God has chosen and loved us. The initiative for our salvation therefore lies with God alone—and our appropriate response to this amazing mystery is awe.

Why did God take pains to accomplish this choosing and saving work on our behalf? God did this for one final purpose: that we, with all the rest of creation, might glorify God and sing of his grace (1:6, 12). Sun, moon, and stars; turtles, tarantulas, and tulips—"all creatures great and small"—join to sing their Maker's praise (see Ps. 19). Even Jesus, God's Son, came to earth to bring back glory to his Father in heaven (John 17:4). Someone once said that to be human is to be one point in the universe where God's goodness receives an echo of gratitude for all the Lord has done. (See also Ps. 8:1-2; Isa. 43:7, 19-21; 62:7; Jer. 13:11.)

Redemption by His Blood

Not wishing to interrupt what he's thinking and saying, Paul continues by stating that God's work of choosing and saving us incurred unbelievable costs. God redeemed our lives through the suffering and death of his very own Son (Eph. 1:7).

Both Jewish and Gentile readers would have caught the significance of Paul's claim here, for redemption has historical parallels in both the Old Testament and in the ancient pagan world. The Jews had their Old Testament "kinsman redeemer," one who recovered a poverty-stricken relative's property rights by paying that person's debt (see Ruth 3-4). And in ancient pagan warfare, high-ranking officials who were taken captive could be bought back and freed by their fellow citizens for a ransom—a redemption—paid to the victors.

As sinners, says Paul, we are not free; we are enslaved to our sinful nature. But Christ has redeemed us; he has paid the price required by God "to fulfill all righteousness" for our sake (Matt. 3:15). In this way Christ has opened the way for us to be reconciled with God (2 Cor. 5:17-21; Col. 1:19-20).

When Jesus came and redeemed his people, a new era began. What excited Paul and ignited his passion was this compelling vision: God's great salvation brings "all things in heaven and on earth" (1:10)—not less than *everything* God has made—together in Jesus Christ. Adam's sin separated us from community with God in paradise; Christ's redemption recovered that blessed relationship for us. Jesus, our Savior, is the Lord and pivot point of history. When Paul thought about what God through Christ had done for him—indeed, for the entire cosmos—he knew that only one response was fitting: "I consider my life worth nothing to me, if only I may . . . complete the task the Lord Jesus has given me—the task of testifying to the gospel of God's grace" (Acts 20:24).

Additional Notes

1:1—As in most of his letters, Paul begins by identifying himself as a "sent one" ("apostle") of God. It's always important for his readers, then and now, to remember that Paul speaks and writes by divine necessity, not by personal choice. Thus his words come with the authority of God.

It is well documented in commentaries and New Testament footnotes that the words "in Ephesus" are not found in some of the earliest and most reliable manuscripts. This helps to explain the letter's minimal personal greetings and apparent design for a general audience—not to mention that Paul does not refer to his earlier two years of service in Ephesus (see Acts 19:10). Most scholars have concluded that the letter was intended for circulation to a number of churches in the region of Ephesus.

1:3—This verse contains three significant expressions. (1) "Every spiritual blessing" refers to every salvation blessing now available to believers through the work of the Holy Spirit. Included are the benefits spelled out in the opening doxology: election to holiness, adoption into God's family, redemption, forgiveness, and so on. (2) "In the heavenly realms," an expression unique to this book of the Bible, appears five times in this letter. This expression refers to the heavenly throne, where Christ is exalted. Every spiritual blessing comes from the one God who reigns from this throne. (3) "In Christ," is a key phrase indicating that spiritual blessings are enjoyed only by those who are united with Christ through faith.

1:9-10—When Paul speaks of "the mystery of [God's] will," this is not a mystery in the sense of a secret teaching known only to a few insiders. For Paul this refers to the counsel of God in working out salvation in human history. While the full mystery of God is too great for our minds to grasp, the mystery of God's design for salvation is now revealed through the coming of Christ, his death, resurrection, and exaltation. Now it is clear what God is up to—bringing "all things in heaven and on earth together under one head, even Christ."

GENERAL DISCUSSION

1. No sooner has Paul given his readers the loaded greeting "Grace and peace to you . . ." than he launches into soaring praise to "the God and Father of our Lord Jesus Christ." Why? What has Paul got to sing about? What effect might such an opening have on his readers?

2. What does it mean to be "blessed . . . in the heavenly realms with every spiritual blessing" (Eph. 1:3)? Make a list of the spiritual blessings you have, and share one or two of your answers with your group.

make me want to know the Lord

3. When it comes to being certain about your salvation, is Ephesians 1:4-6 reassuring to you? Explain. Do you have any problem with the teaching of these verses? Explain.

Because of his Love

Yes

4. Suppose someone curious about Christianity asked you, "What is God doing in the world, anyway?" How would you answer? Compare your answer with Ephesians 1:10. What evidence do you see that God is making progress in bringing "all things . . . together under . . . Christ"?

5. Why is God's revelation called a "mystery" (Eph. 1:9)? (See also Col. 1:25-29.) To whom has God made this "mystery" known? What are the implications of this revelation for the church? What relevance does this revelation have in our North American culture today?

SMALL GROUP SESSION IDEAS

Opening (10-15 minutes)

Pray/Worship—Open your first session of this study with a prayer for God's wisdom and guidance as you look to the Scriptures to grow in faith. Thank God for bringing you together for this Bible study, and since part of this session's focus is on praise, consider singing together an opening praise song to the Lord, such as "Father, I Adore You," "Praise to the Lord, the Almighty," or "To God Be the Glory."

Share—If your group is used to meeting together, you'll want to take some time to catch up on how things have been going since you last met. If some or all of you haven't been part of this group before, take time to introduce yourselves and perhaps each share something about yourself that you'd like the others to know. For starters, you may want to note the expectations you have as you begin this study of Ephesians.

Focus—The focus question in each session aims to help you concentrate on a central truth in the lesson material and how it affects you. Ask yourself the following question as you begin this session: *What does God's grace in Christ mean to me?*

Growing (35-40 minutes)

Read (Optional)—You may want to read Ephesians 1:1-10 together (as well as the study-guide notes) before moving into a discussion time.

Discuss—While working through the General Discussion questions for this lesson, you may wish to include some of the following process questions as they fit in with your discussion.

- What have you learned about "grace and peace" in this lesson?
- What can you do to help God bring about more peace and blessing in your personal life? In your small group? In your community? In this world?
- What institutions or organizations are you involved in that give evidence of the Lord's work in this world? What kinds of service do these organizations offer?

Goalsetting (5 minutes)

Try to work on the following goal in the coming week:

- Here's what I want to do to help God bring about more peace and blessing in this world:

Closing (10-15 minutes)

Preparing for Prayer—This is a time for sharing praise items and concerns that you'd like others to bring before God in prayer for you, both now and in the coming week. You may also want to ask for prayers for God's help in meeting the goal you've set during this session.

Prayer—Close your meeting with prayer, asking the Lord to help you live lives of praise and service for his glory. Everyone may join in with prayer concerns and praises. Then ask for God's blessing and guidance in the coming weeks as you study Ephesians together, seeking to learn and grow in faith. Before parting, you may also wish to sing together a familiar praise song like "King of Kings and Lord of Lords" or "Praise God, from Whom All Blessings Flow."

To know Christ is to be greatly blessed— and the best is yet to come.

2

EPHESIANS 1:11-23

Sealed with the Spirit to Hope in Christ

Ephesians 1:11-23

11In him we were also chosen, having been predestined according to the plan of him who works out everything in conformity with the purpose of his will, 12in order that we, who were the first to hope in Christ, might be for the praise of his glory. 13And you also were included in Christ when you heard the word of truth, the gospel of your salvation. Having believed, you were marked in him with a seal, the promised Holy Spirit, 14who is a deposit guaranteeing our inheritance until the redemption of those who are God's possession—to the praise of his glory.

15For this reason, ever since I heard about your faith in the Lord Jesus and your love for all the saints, 16I have not stopped giving thanks for you, remembering you in my prayers. 17I keep asking that the God of our Lord Jesus Christ, the glorious Father, may give you the Spirit of wisdom and revelation, so that you may know him better. 18I pray also that the eyes of your heart may be enlightened in order that you may know the hope to which he has called you, the riches of his glorious inheritance in the saints, 19and his incomparably great power for us who believe. That power is like the working of his mighty strength, 20which he exerted in Christ when he raised him from the dead and seated him at his right hand in the heavenly realms, 21far above all rule and authority, power and dominion, and every title that can be given, not only in the present age but also in the one to come. 22And God placed all things under his feet and appointed him to be head over everything for the church, 23which is his body, the fullness of him who fills everything in every way.

Our Spiritual Inheritance—in History

From beginning to end the Bible proclaims that the hottest piece of news is what the one true God has been doing in all of history. God has been deliberately active from "before the creation of the world" (Eph. 1:4), working out "everything in conformity with the purpose of his will" (1:11). Everything!

This profound, sweeping claim calls for deep, Spirit-led pondering that can vitally transform the way we view our lives.

No detail of my life, your life, or anyone else's life escapes God's sovereign attention and control. Every circumstance serves as malleable clay for God to use in shaping us into persons of holiness.

Note the grand sweep of divine activity in the lives of all who belong to God. God "chose us" (1:5, 11) and determined to save us according to a purposeful, established plan. God has a purpose for his creation and for each person who belongs to him. And that purpose is integrally linked to Christ, God's Son, so that we "might be for the praise of [God's] glory" (1:12, 14). God has made and remade us for his glory. Our single pursuit, as Jesus reminds us, must be to live in such a way that we bring glory to our Father in heaven (Matt. 5:13-16). What an arresting thought for many of us today who sometimes foolishly act as if everything revolves around us!

In salvation history the Lord set about methodically to bring his people home again. God first chose the Jews, who therefore became "the first to hope in Christ" (Eph. 1:12). Paul was among them, and, with others, he brought the good news of salvation to Jews wherever he preached the gospel (see Acts 11:19; 13:5; Rom. 1:16). Then he and others proclaimed the same message to Gentiles, who "also were included in Christ when [they] heard the word of truth, the gospel of . . . salvation" (Eph. 1:13). Now all people, both Jews and Gentiles together, share in the same inheritance.

Sealed with the Holy Spirit

What God began to do through Jesus Christ now continues through the work of the Holy Spirit, who applies Christ's work to every believer. The goal for everyone who belongs to God is clear: each one must grow to know God better (1:17). The Holy Spirit works in each of us to bring us to fuller maturity as God's people.

In this work the Holy Spirit functions as a "seal" for our benefit (1:13; see also 4:30). Seals accomplish three purposes:

- to attest that a work is genuine
- to signify ownership
- to secure the contents of a container

Each of these purposes is important for us in connection with the Holy Spirit. *First,* the Spirit verifies that we are God's called-out children. When our hearts become weak and our souls become so tired that we wonder whether God's promises are true or whether God really loves us, the Spirit assures us and supplies peace and power to our anxious souls.

Second, the Spirit attests that we belong only to God, that we are indeed "God's possession" (1:14). When we, being vulnerable to Satan's lures and lies, become tempted to imagine we belong to someone or something besides God—such as the corporation we work for, the nation we live in, or even the devil himself—then the Holy Spirit reminds us who we really are and to whom we really belong. We are God's—and God's alone.

Third, the Spirit makes us secure forever. The Greek word *arrabon* referring to the Spirit in 1:14 means "installment, pledge, deposit." So the gift of the Spirit is like a down payment verifying that God will continue the work begun in us until the final day of redemption (1:14). The Spirit is our daily assurance, amid all the twists and turns in our lives, that God will see us through.

A Warm, Unceasing Prayer

With the transitional phrase "For this reason" (1:15) Paul notes that the grand theology he's been discussing has led to some wonderful practical results in the lives of his Christian friends. Paul says he continually thanks God for the way these believers have put their trust in Jesus and shown their love not just for one another but "for all the saints."

Grand theology is important, to be sure. But good theological thinking must give shape to practical living.

As he expresses his thanks for the Ephesians' faithful living, Paul adds that he keeps asking the "God of our Lord Jesus Christ" to supply "the Spirit of wisdom and revelation" so that his readers may come to know God better (1:17). A person will never come to know Jesus as Savior and Lord by "trying real hard" to believe. To believe in God and to grow in the knowledge of God requires dependence on the Lord and his Spirit, who initiates faith and maintains it in the believer's heart.

Paul pleads further that the "eyes" of his readers' "heart may be enlightened" to know hope (1:18). Paul is referring to the heart here as the center of one's being, the seat of one's will, knowledge, and understanding. The "Spirit of wisdom and revelation" comes to live in the heart to enlighten and transform a person through and through. So Paul's plea is that his readers continue growing in the knowledge of God so they can hope in the Lord with all their heart, so they can have a lively hope in God and in all God's promises for their future. Day by day they can grow more confident as they face their future in

Christ—and thus be less paralyzed by fear—so that they can continue living for him.

The hope Paul is speaking about is not some vague cross-your-fingers sort of hope that things might turn out all right someday. Christian hope is anchored in the actions of God in history, including the sure promise that God is completing what has already begun in Christ.

Jesus, History's Absolute Lord

With that sure hope in mind, Paul concludes this part of his letter with a breathtaking recital of God's amazing work in Christ. Raised by God from the dead, Jesus is now seated in honor at God's right hand, exalted "far above all rule and authority, power and dominion, and every title that can be given, not only in the present age, but also in the age to come" (1:21; see also Matt. 28:19-20).

Jesus wields this awesome power for the welfare of all who belong to him. He's the "head over everything for the [sake of his] church," and the church, "his body," is the awesome "fullness of him who fills everything in every way" (1:22-23; see Matt. 16:18). What a rich relationship between Christ and his church!

As believers, we need never fear about the present status of our Savior and Lord, nor of our security in him. As the Heidelberg Catechism says, in God's care "we can be patient when things go against us, thankful when things go well, and for the future we can have good confidence" (Q&A 28), knowing the best is yet to come. Because of all God has done for us in Christ, who has "the whole world in his hands," we can live—and love—for him in Christian hope. (See also Matt. 6:25-34; John 10:28-29.)

Additional Notes

1:11—It's impressive to note how Paul emphasizes the limitless scope of God's saving work through Jesus Christ. Again and again in Ephesians 1 Paul uses a form of the word *panta* (meaning "every," "everything," or "all things") to describe the extent of our salvation blessings and of God's powerful grace: "every spiritual blessing" (1:3); "all wisdom and understanding" (1:8); "to bring all things . . . together under one head" (1:10); "him who works out everything" (1:11); "far above all rule and authority . . . and every title" (1:21); "God placed all things under his feet and appointed him to be head over everything" (1:22); "the fullness of him who fills everything in every way" (1:23).

1:12—For the second time in this opening doxology Paul refers to the purpose of God's work as "the praise of his glory" (see also 1:6, 14). As Markus Barth notes in his commentary on Ephesians (in the *Anchor Bible Series*), "Paul wanted to make clear that not only the root and means of God's decision and work are located in God himself, but also their purpose." It is by God's grace alone (and "according to his good pleasure"—1:9) that we are saved, and God's purpose in so doing is to create a people who will bring him glory and praise (see Deut. 26:19; Isa. 43:7, 21; 62:7; Jer. 13:11; 1 Pet. 2:9).

1:17—The NIV correctly translates "Spirit" in this verse as a reference to the Holy Spirit (see NIV footnote for alternate, literally "a spirit"). Paul's request was not for the Ephesian believers to receive a second infusion of the Spirit "but for the indwelling Spirit whom they have already received to give them further wisdom and revelation," says Gordon Fee in *God's Empowering Presence: The Holy Spirit in the Letters of Paul.*

1:20-21—Paul says that Christ has been exalted above every type of authority that exists in the universe. By "rule and authority, power and dominion, and every title that can be given" (1:21), the apostle refers not only to earthly powers but also to the powers of the angelic or spirit world, including that of the demons (see also 3:10; 6:12; Col. 1:16; 2:10).

1:22-23—Notice the distinction Paul makes in 1:23 between the church ("his body") as "fullness" and the filling of "everything in every way." Christ "fills everything" in the sense that his mighty presence is everywhere and his power is over all. The church is his "fullness" in a special way because it is the body in which the benefits and gifts of his power are received and enjoyed. (For a helpful discussion on this matter, see Herman Ridderbos's presentation in *Paul: An Outline of His Theology,* pp. 387-92.)

GENERAL DISCUSSION

1. In our Scripture for this lesson Paul moves from declaring God's praises (Eph. 1:11-14) to asking God for more blessing (1:15-23). What's the connection between these activities? Further, what's the connection between "grand theology" and practical living? In each case, what effect would it have

on your life if you were preoccupied with one over the other?

2. Today it is increasingly common for individuals as well as businesses to write "mission statements" that express their sense of calling or purpose. How might Ephesians 1:11-12 influence your personal mission statement? How might 1:13-14 influence your church's mission statement?

3. In Ephesians 1:18-19 Paul prays for spiritual enlightenment that will raise his readers' awareness about three matters: hope, riches, and power. What difference would each of these make for your (personal) faith and for the church's faith today if you (and the church at large) grew in these areas?

4. How is the church ordinarily portrayed in our society today? Give examples from books, movies, documentaries, news media, politics, and so on. Compare these examples with the portrayal we find in Ephesians 1:22-23. What difference should this biblical teaching make for our sense of mission in the world?

SMALL GROUP SESSION IDEAS

Opening (10-15 minutes)

Pray—Open your session with prayer, asking for the Lord's presence in your hearts as you study the importance of the Holy Spirit and our hope in Christ.

Share—Share how you're doing on the goal you set in lesson 1. To lead into your study for this lesson, use this time also to review briefly what you learned in the previous lesson.

Focus—Ask yourself the following focus question as you begin this session: *What is the extent of my hope in Christ?*

Growing (35-40 minutes)
Read (Optional)—You may want to read Ephesians 1:11-23 together. You may also wish to read or review the study guide notes before moving into your discussion time.

Discuss—While working through the General Discussion questions for this lesson, you may want to include some of the following process questions as they fit in with your discussion.

- In this lesson what have you learned about being sealed with the Holy Spirit?
- How does this knowledge about the Holy Spirit affect your hope in Christ?
- In what ways can you put this hope to work for Christ in your personal life? In the work of the church?
- How much power do you believe is available to you in Christ in order to be a part of his mission in this world?

Goalsetting (5 minutes)
Try working toward the following goal in the coming week:

- I want to grow in my sense of hope through Christ's Spirit, and here's how I would like to put that hope to work, in my Lord's power:

Closing (10-15 minutes)
Preparing for Prayer—Share items for the group to bring before God in prayer, both now and in the coming week.

Prayer—Close your meeting with prayer, thanking God for the seal of the Holy Spirit and the hope we can have to live forever in the power of Christ. Everyone may join in with prayer concerns and praises. Before parting till your next meeting, you might also like to sing some songs like these: "Spirit of the

Living God," "Dwell in Me, O Blessed Spirit," "O Worship the King," "From Ocean unto Ocean."

Group Service Project (Optional)

You and your group may be interested in a cause that looks ahead to God's coming kingdom in all its fullness, when "all things" under the authority of Christ will be fully redeemed and restored—"to the praise of [God's] glory" (Eph. 1:14, 21-23). Check with local health, welfare, political action, denominational, and environmental agencies for ideas and help in getting started.

For example, you might help in a local immunization clinic, a blood drive, or a food program; clean up a roadway, waterway, or disaster site; work toward human rights, legal justice, community safety, literacy and basic skills education, biblical literacy, acceptance and education of persons with impairments or disabilities, responsible medical research, preservation of wildlife, proper use of land, cleaner air and water—the list goes on and on. Every area of our lives and of this world is under Christ's authority, and he calls us to seek God's kingdom and righteousness as we live in this world (Deut. 20:19-20; 22:6-7; Ps. 24:1-2; Matt. 6:33; Luke 12:31; Eph. 1:9-10, 21-23; 4:1, 17-24; Rev. 22:1-2).

"There but for the grace of God go I. . . ."

3

EPHESIANS 2:1-10

A New Creation—by Grace

Ephesians 2:1-10

1As for you, you were dead in your
transgressions and sins, 2in which you
used to live when you followed the ways
of this world and of the ruler of the king-
dom of the air, the spirit who is now at
work in those who are disobedient. 3All of
us also lived among them at one time,
gratifying the cravings of our sinful nature
and following its desires and thoughts.
Like the rest, we were by nature objects of
wrath. 4But because of his great love for us,
God, who is rich in mercy, 5made us alive
with Christ even when we were dead in
transgressions—it is by grace you have
been saved. 6And God raised us up with
Christ and seated us with him in the heav-
enly realms in Christ Jesus, 7in order that
in the coming ages he might show the
incomparable riches of his grace,
expressed in his kindness to us in Christ
Jesus. 8For it is by grace you have been
saved, through faith—and this not from
yourselves, it is the gift of God—9not by
works, so that no one can boast. 10For we
are God's workmanship, created in Christ
Jesus to do good works, which God pre-
pared in advance for us to do.

Sobering Evidence

Three sobering, arresting memories spring to mind as I reflect on this passage:

- A college junior once acknowledged to me his long pattern of alcohol use. Gradually he had become addicted. He had begun drinking in seventh grade, and by tenth grade he was totally hooked. "I tried and tried to quit," he lamented, "but I found myself powerless to do anything about it. My will was as drunk as I was." It was no longer possible for him to say no to alcohol.

- A young man, caught up in a pattern of deceit and flagrant lawbreaking, was arrested and wrote me one of the most depressing letters I have ever received. Penitent and remorseful for the pain he had inflicted on his family and friends, he cried out, "I have lost so much because of the terrible things I have done. I find myself screaming Psalm 51 every night. Does God hear me through my endless tears and sobbing? Chaplain, I am sorry. I do not write for your sympathy—in fact, I don't want any sympathy. I don't even want to send this letter. As I look back and reread it, I ask myself why I even wrote it. Lord Jesus Christ, have mercy upon me, a miserable sinner."

- G. K. Chesterton once said that the Christian teaching about sin and evil does not even require faith—it is provable by evidential data.

The Human Morass of Sin and Evil

Throughout history, people have often claimed that we humans should be able to live together politely and well and to create a just and good society. Some optimistic scholars have even said that in our heart of hearts we human beings really are good.

Such optimists are usually willing to concede that none of us is perfect—at least not yet. We're still crippled by ignorance, stupidity, and a bad environment. Until now these factors have limited our ability to act well, they say. But we humans now have the capacity to correct our flaws: by education we can remedy ignorance; through selective human breeding we can weed out stupidity and weaknesses caused by genetic defects; by cleaning up our neighborhoods and environment we can put everyone in a better frame of mind to live rightly.

The apostle Paul is a lot less hopeful about the human prospect: at the core of our existence we are not nice people. In fact, we're sinful through and through—Paul's word for us is *nekros*: we're "dead," like corpses walking around. And we're in desperate straits because of the sin that pervades each one of us. No matter how well we've mastered or how high we've risen to establish our prestige, we're still in a dreadful state. And the sickest among us are those who try to hide from themselves and deceive others, putting on the thin coat of respectability and pretending they're different from others.

Paul says we once "followed the ways of this world" (2:2). In the original Greek text the verb for "followed" means literally "to walk around" (*peripateo*), and it's a favorite metaphor of both Paul and John in the New Testament. *Peripateo* can be used to describe the regular but steady progress of a redeemed person trying to live by the promises and commands of God (see Rom. 6:4; Eph. 2:10; 4:1). But this verb can also describe the habits of unredeemed people who live "according to the flesh," or "by the standards of this world"—that is, disobediently (see 1 Cor. 3:3; 2 Cor. 10:2). Paul's point here is that every believer, prior to God's rescue, once lived by the pattern, principles, and motives of "this world" (*kosmou toutou*). We were continually seduced by its evils, and we fell prey to its sick impulses and enticements. Not until we were remade in Christ did we begin to "walk around" or really live as God has intended (see 2:10).

Before following Christ, we followed "the ruler of the kingdom of the air" (2:2). The Greek word for "ruler" (*archonta*) denotes "one who is chief, first, highest." And the phrase "kingdom of the air" refers to a popular idea in Paul's day that while the gods were in heaven and humans were on earth, the air in between was inhabited by spirits, some of them evil. Paul refers to this notion to remind his readers that they were held captive to evil influences and spirits before Christ came to free them.

A God of Wrath?

Continually "gratifying the cravings of our sinful nature and following its desires and thoughts," we became "by nature objects of wrath" (2:3). Note how in this verse Paul turns from "you" to "we": he includes himself in the miserable plight in which all humans find themselves. Duped by the evil one and enslaved by lustful cravings from which we *could not* free ourselves even if we wanted to, we received our due consequence: the wrath of God.

Try talking today about God expressing anger and wrath toward human beings, and most people raise their eyebrows, as if to say, "You can't be serious! A God of wrath?" After all, God in his very nature is one who loves and is merciful. How could God display something so hostile as wrath?

The Greek word for wrath (*orge*) literally means "to teem, to abound, to swell (with moisture) as it ripens, to become passionate and excited." So Paul is saying here that the consistent, regular wrongdoing of human beings has evoked a consistent, intensifying response within God. The Lord has become fully ripened with righteous anger toward his creatures. In God there is nothing fanatical, arbitrary, or out of character in this matter. Our continuing human evil has simply gradually increased the heat of God's wrath. Further, it's important to know that along with being loving and merciful, God is also holy. This means the Lord is wholly opposed to evil; evil has no place or standing in the presence of the one holy God. One day God will unleash his wrath on all evil, but for the time being, out of love and mercy, God is holding back so that we may repent and seek forgiveness and new life through Christ (see Col. 1:21-23; 2 Pet. 3:9-10; Rev. 16-20).

We human beings cannot begin to gauge the magnificence of God's amazing love until we begin to visualize, through eyes of faith, the full blast of God's hot displeasure against our wrongdoing. If we discard the teaching about God's furious wrath (against evil), we will eventually lose sight of the splendor of divine grace and forgiveness.

"But . . . God . . ."

What a startling interruption Paul makes to this sobering litany when he writes next, "But . . . God . . ." (2:4)! Says Martin Lloyd-Jones: "These two words, in and of themselves, in a sense contain the whole of the gospel." When our situation was bleak and utterly hopeless, God, in Christ, did for us what we could never do for ourselves: he saved us (2:5; see Rom. 5:6-11). God's intervention made all the difference.

What has God done for us? Three things: "made us alive *with* Christ" (Eph. 2:5), "raised us up *with* Christ," and "seated us *with* him in the heavenly realms" (2:6). Note the daring claims here about our present status, since we are rescued by God. Paul is saying that Christ is not only *for* us but is also *with* us—and we are *with* him!

Again and again throughout his letters Paul underscores the close relationship between believers and their Lord. The apostle generously sprinkles phrases such as "in the Lord," "in Christ," "in him," and so on—no fewer than 164 times in his writings. And here Paul uses the preposition *with* to indicate the unbreakable bond between Christ and all who belong to him. We have been resurrected with Christ; we now have a new life with him; and we have even begun to reign with him.

Contrary to the message of some hymns that say our triumph with Christ is still far off, Paul says that salvation for us is *now*. It has already begun. Jesus, having completed his saving work and now ruling at the right hand of honor and power with his Father in heaven, has seated us there with himself! The coming age, in which we will live with Christ and reign with him forever, is only a fuller and more intense continuation of our salvation that has already begun. In Christ and by the power of the Spirit we can begin to enjoy and exercise our "spiritual [salvation] blessings" even now (1:3). Just one example of this is the power we can have, by the Holy Spirit, to let go of our worries and stop trying to run things in our own lives so that God can use us for his purposes—right where we are (see Matt. 6:25-34; Phil. 4:4-9, 12-13).

Why has God done all this for us? Paul uses four phrases to describe God's nature and to clarify God's motive. God has "great love for us," is "rich in mercy" toward us (2:4), shows us "the incomparable riches of his grace," and has expressed "kindness to us" (2:7). Our sin and God's resulting anger toward us never have the last word in the relationship God maintains with us. God the Judge has become our Father. When our claim to God's mercy and love was fully spent, God—inexplicably and beyond our ability to understand—loved us by grace alone.

Wise people today, in addition to meditating on their sin and evil, do well, says the Puritan Richard Rogers, to cherish faith daily "by taking comfort and great delight in the great benefit of our redemption by Christ." How often do we truly need to meditate—as former slave-trader-turned-Christian-hymn-writer John Newton put it—on the amazing grace of God that saves wretches like us!

God's Workmanship

As if to build toward a crescendo, Paul stunningly reverses the word order in 2:10 (in the Greek text), placing heavy emphasis on the last word of his phrase as follows: "For of him we are a workmanship." (Most English translations follow this pattern.) The word translated as "workmanship" is *poiema,* from which we derive our word *poem.* Paul declares, in effect, "Behold, what a specimen of divine poetry each of us is—a masterpiece of God's work!" In other writings, as in this verse, Paul describes us as newly "created in Christ Jesus" (2:10; see 2 Cor. 5:17; Gal. 6:15).

In my work as a pastor among college-age young people, I often heard refrains like these: "I'm not really worth much"; "I don't think very much of myself"; "Who cares about me?"; "What am I good for?" Lack of good self-esteem is epidemic.

The solution, however, is not to be found in fighting one's way toward looking good—dieting, exercising to stay in shape, dressing fashionably. Nor in fighting to prove oneself smarter—high grades, entrance into a top graduate school, landing a fine job. Nor in money—having a huge income, driving expensive cars, flaunting status or possessions. Nor in worldly power—pushing others around, wielding influence through buyouts and corrupt networking. People who try to establish their identity and secure their worth by their own power and ability eventually tire out. And they lose whenever someone sharper, smarter, or more influential comes along.

The key to good self-esteem lies here: *We are God's masterpiece,* originally made by the one God and Creator of all, and now remade in Christ. We are loved, accepted, forgiven, and made secure forever—all because God has been, is, and always will be good to us.

Additional Notes

2:3—The apostle declares that "we were by nature objects [literally 'children'] of wrath," thus drawing a contrast between what we were "by nature" and what we have become "by grace" (2:5). Scholars often suggest that we understand Paul's statement here as a summary of his argument in Romans 5:12-19 about our solidarity in sin through the fall of Adam. As expressed in the Heidelberg Catechism, "this fall has so poisoned our nature that we are born sinners—corrupt from conception on" (Q&A 7).

2:7—In this verse Paul states the purpose of our salvation. Earlier he cites the raising and exalting of Christ as a demonstration of God's "incomparably great power" (1:19). But in raising and exalting believers (2:6), God demonstrates "the incomparable riches of his grace" (2:7). "As living evidences of his kindness we shall point people away and beyond ourselves to him to whom we owe our salvation," writes John Stott in *God's New Society.*

GENERAL DISCUSSION

1. Many people in our culture today believe that education is the solution to all social problems. The assumption is that "to know better is to do better." In the light of Ephesians 2:1-10, how would you evaluate that belief, and what would you offer as a Christian alternative?

2. On the basis of Ephesians 2:1-5, in what way is the notion of "free will" a myth? How might these verses affect the way you pray about your (and the church's) witness to people who are spiritually lost?

3. The preceding comments state, "Wise people don't slight sin. They pay attention to it." How do we (or should we) "pay attention" to sin in our lives? In our worship? Is enough attention paid to sin in our church communities today? Why or why not?

4. What does it mean to you that you are "made alive with Christ," "raised up with Christ" and "seated with him in the heavenly realms"? (Along with Eph. 2:4-10, see Rom. 6:1-14; Col. 3:1-4.) How does this relate to being "God's workmanship" (Eph. 2:10)?

SMALL GROUP SESSION IDEAS

Opening (10-15 minutes)

Pray—Open with prayer, asking the God "who is rich in mercy" to guide your study about sin, grace, and our being new creatures in Christ.

Share—Share with each other how you're doing on the goals you've set in previous lessons.

Focus—Reflect on the following focus question as you begin this session: *What does being re-created in Christ mean to me?*

Growing (35-40 minutes)

Read (Optional)—You may want to read Ephesians 2:1-10 together (along with the study guide notes) before moving into your discussion time.

Discuss—While working through the General Discussion questions for this lesson, you may want to include some of the following process questions as they fit in with your discussion.

What have you learned about sin and grace in this lesson?

- In what ways do you "pay attention" to sin in your own life? In your personal worship time with God?

- What does it mean to you to have new life through grace in Christ? What can (or do) you do to show others that you have this new life?

Goalsetting (5 minutes)
Try working on the following goal as a result of this session:

- I want to apply myself to show others the new life I have in Christ. Here's what I want to do, in the strength of the Holy Spirit:

Closing (10-15 minutes)
Preparing for Prayer—Share items that you'd like the others in your group to bring before God in prayer for you.

Prayer—Close with prayer, asking God to help each of you recognize the sin in your lives and to help you live grateful new lives in Christ. Everyone may join in with prayer concerns and praises. Before parting, you may wish to sing "Lord, I Want to Be a Christian" or another familiar song about living for Christ.

Group Study/Work Project (Optional)
Perhaps your group would like to learn about and help to shape social programs and public policy from a Christian perspective. You could gather information by contacting your church's political action committee; a Christian AIDS-awareness group; Christian social help or family service organizations; your denomination's domestic relief organization; your local, state, or congressional representatives; or other sources. To begin, you might assign one or two group members to search out information and possibilities for the group's involvement; then at a later meeting you could review the gathered information and decide on an activity to get involved in.

Group Study Project (Optional)
Some or all of you may wish to read *Not the Way It's Supposed to Be: A Breviary of Sin* by Cornelius Plantinga, Jr. (Eerdmans, 1995), and report on its main points during a later session (such as lesson 7).

How could any believer even hint that another doesn't belong?

4

EPHESIANS 2:11-22

Hostility Erased

Ephesians 2:11-22

11Therefore, remember that formerly
you who are Gentiles by birth and called
"uncircumcised" by those who call them-
selves "the circumcision" (that done in the
body by the hands of men)—12remember
that at that time you were separate from
Christ, excluded from citizenship in Israel
and foreigners to the covenants of the
promise, without hope and without God
in the world. 13But now in Christ Jesus you
who once were far away have been
brought near through the blood of Christ.

14For he himself is our peace, who has
made the two one and has destroyed the
barrier, the dividing wall of hostility, 15by
abolishing in his flesh the law with its
commandments and regulations. His
purpose was to create in himself one new
man out of the two, thus making peace,
16and in this one body to reconcile both
of them to God through the cross, by
which he put to death their hostility. 17He
came and preached peace to you who were
far away and peace to those who were
near. 18For through him we both have
access to the Father by one Spirit.

19Consequently, you are no longer
foreigners and aliens, but fellow citizens
with God's people and members of God's
household, 20built on the foundation of
the apostles and prophets, with Christ
Jesus himself as the chief cornerstone. 21In
him the whole building is joined together
and rises to become a holy temple in the
Lord. 22And in him you too are being built
together to become a dwelling in which
God lives by his Spirit.

Just My Imagination?

Is it my imagination, or is intolerance heating up again these days? Often it seems that despite decades of efforts of urging people to come together and seeking to understand and accept one another, divisions rage both outside and within the body of Christ. We pit ourselves against one another and arm ourelves with arguments—sometimes even with weapons and terrorism—in misguided attempts to get our point across. In many ways it seems we've become a culture of *us versus them:* conservative versus liberal, right versus left, capitalist versus socialist, rural versus urban, NRA versus gun control, pro-choice versus pro-life, male versus female, black versus white, gay versus straight, single versus married—the fault lines are everywhere.

Isn't the work of Christ and the Holy Spirit supposed to change all that? Yes—and God calls us to work *with* him in this great kingdom expansion.

Alienation and Separation

Paul begins his next section of Ephesians with "Therefore" (Eph. 2:11), because what he has to say next is a direct consequence of what he has just affirmed in 2:1-10. Since everyone in Christ has been saved by God's goodness alone and each of us is God's workmanship, none of us is or may be treated as an outcast or alien—no matter who we are or what part of society we belong to. We now belong, completely and forever, to the household of God. We form the temple in which God is pleased to dwell.

Ancient society, like ours, was shot through with divisions. Free people held slaves and looked down on them as inferiors—chunks of flesh to do menial work. Men looked down on women and considered them inferior. Greeks cherished their Hellenist culture and deemed all others barbaric. Jews, chosen by God and distinguished from other nations by the mark of circumcision, sneered at Gentiles, labeling them unclean and uncircumcised.

Gentiles were clearly unwelcome within the inner sanctum of the Jewish temple. A wall with "No Trespassing" signs prevented all non-Jews from proceeding any farther than the outer Court of the Gentiles.

But far worse than any social ostracism they may have felt, the Gentiles were spiritual outsiders, "foreigners to the covenants of the promise" (2:12). Before Jesus came, only the Jews had received the covenant of God. Gentiles had not received God's law, the priesthood, the covenant promises, and the Lord's guidance and protection (see Deut. 32:9-14). So in that sense they were "without hope and without God" (Eph. 2:12).

Signs of hopelessness were everywhere. The ancient Greek dramatist Sophocles once said, "The best thing to happen to a man is never to be born; the next best thing is to be born and die prematurely." A Roman, expressing his despair, composed this epitaph to be placed on his tomb: "There was a time when I was not; then I became; now I no longer am. I do not care." These voices have modern echoes.

We should note, however, that although the Gentiles were "foreigners to the covenants," it was always God's purpose to include them. Even in God's first covenant promise to Abraham we read, "All peoples on earth will be blessed through you" (Gen. 12:3). As we learn in Paul's next few lines, it took Christ to fulfill these words of God's promise.

The Dividing Wall Dismantled

The Gentiles, once considered "far away" (2:13; see Isa. 57:9; Acts 2:39)—a rabbinic term of reproach toward Gentiles—"have been brought near through the blood of Christ" (Eph. 2:13). In Christ the Gentiles' spiritual alienation has come to an end. For Jesus breaks down "the dividing wall of hostility" (2:14) and restores peace among all who belong to God.

When Christ died on the cross, he abolished "in his flesh the law with its commandments and regulations" (2:15). The great wall that Jews had set up to keep their distance from Gentiles was the intricate system of ceremonial feasts, sacrifices, and standards of cleanliness. But all this had now come to an end; Christ made the final sacrifice. By his death all people now have access to God's grace.

Note that Christ not only brings peace but also "*is* our peace" (2:14; see Mic. 5:5). The peace of Christ is so thorough and pervasive that it has created an entirely new community, "one new man out of the two" (Eph. 2:15). And this peace is so much more than the elimination of hostility. It is not simply the absence of something negative. It's *shalom,* which is far richer and more positive. My Hebrew dictionary defines *shalom* as "completeness, soundness, welfare, peace." *Shalom* is what God intends for his creation; it's the "flourishing of creation" with justice and delight, as Cornelius Plantinga, Jr., puts it in his book *Not the Way It's Supposed to Be.*

Paul's Jewish readers would have understood the immense depth and breadth of the term *shalom*; his Gentile readers perhaps less so. But the same Christ "came and preached" *shalom* to both (2:17).

To both Jews and Gentiles Jesus provided "access to the Father by one Spirit" (2:18). The word for "access" (*prosagoge*) occurs only three times in the New Testament, and in each instance the word refers to the believer's ready entrance into God's presence. In ancient society a *prosagogeus* was a highly placed court official who led guests into the presence of the king and introduced them to him. The *prosagogeus* brought them near and gave them the privilege of entrance. Christ does this for each and every believer, both Gentile and Jew. None has a right to come by himself or herself; only through Christ's blood and "by one Spirit" are we brought again into God's holy presence and welcomed (2:18).

Citizens, Household, Holy Temple

In 2:19-22 Paul uses three metaphors to summarize his discussion about the deep unity Christ came to bring. "Foreigners and aliens" have been transformed into *"fellow citizens"* with God's people; strangers now belong to *"God's household"* (2:19); and what once were separate, clashing, unfitting elements have now been sculpted into "a *holy temple* in the Lord" (2:21).

With a strong transitional phrase that means "Wherefore therefore" ("Consequently" in NIV—2:19), Paul aims to underscore the truth of this transformation. His thought seems to be "If all that I have been explaining here is true—and it most certainly is—then, as surely as night follows day, Gentiles and Jews are related to one another in a manner that is constructive, peaceable, harmonious, and utterly non-alienating to any person or group. All of us together are now citizens of a single commonwealth, members of one family, a building in which God himself has taken up residence."

The Greek word for "city" is *polis*, and for "citizen," *polites*. A citizen was a full member of a city or state. Foreigners and aliens (*xenoi* and *paroikoi*), though permitted to live in the city and to work there, clearly were second-class. They had no protection under the law, could be expelled at any time, and had no rights of appeal. They didn't fully belong.

Paul is saying that when Jesus came, he established a whole new commonwealth of subjects who reside within the boundaries of his nation and belong to him as full citizens. All of us who believe in Christ have the rights and privileges of full citizenship in this commonwealth.

But our relationship to God is even richer and more intimate than being citizens of a commonwealth. We are members of "God's household," the family of God. Jesus Christ, God's firstborn Son, and we, God's adopted children, are treated as full members of the same household—within the strong embrace of divine grace and love. (See also Rom. 8:15-17.)

Together, Jewish and Gentile believers now form a structure so stunning that God is pleased to take up residence in it. The church is "built on the foundation [that is, the teachings] of the apostles and prophets." And Christ himself is the "cornerstone," chief among all the stones in the whole structure, the anchor, foundation, and direction setter for all the rest.

What vivid word pictures these are to describe God's people, now gathered into a community in which the Lord is pleased to reside, with its pieces from all nations fitting so wonderfully together! Considering all this, how can anyone who belongs to Jesus even hint that another of Christ's followers doesn't really fit or belong?

GENERAL DISCUSSION

1. How would you respond to someone who said, "We are New Testament Christians. Why do we have to sing the Psalms in church and hear sermons on the Old Testament? And why read the law if Christ has 'abolished' it (Eph. 2:15)?"

2. How do you respond to the question "Is it my imagination, or is intolerance heating up again these days?" What divisions or hostilities do you see or experience in the Christian community today?

3. Are there barriers in your church that may prevent some newcomers or fellow members from feeling like "fellow citizens" (Eph. 2:19)? Give one or two examples. What can you do to help break down those barriers and promote peace and unity in Christ?

4. Reread Paul's prayer in Ephesians 1:18-19. How might Ephesians 2 contribute to the enlightenment Paul desires for his readers? Having studied both parts of Ephesians 2, do you feel motivated by God's revelations there? How and why?

SMALL GROUP SESSION IDEAS

Opening (10-15 minutes)

Pray—Begin your meeting with a time of prayer, asking the Spirit for insight into reconciliation and healing as you study about God's removal of hostilities to create a new people in Christ.

Share—Share with each other how you're doing on the goals you've set in the past few lessons. Now may also be a good time to share information you may have gathered if you're working on the "Group Study/Work Project" suggested in lesson 3.

Focus—Keep the following question in mind as you work through this session: *What does the breaking down of barriers in the church mean to me?*

Growing (35-40 minutes)

Read (Optional)—You may want to read Ephesians 2:11-22 together (along with the study guide notes) before moving into your discussion time.

Discuss—As you work through the General Discussion questions for this lesson, you may want to include some of the following process questions as they fit in with your discussion.

- What have you learned in this lesson about God's work of breaking down hostilities through Christ?
- List a few examples of divisions and hostilities that you've seen broken (or breaking) down in your church and/or small group. How have these changes helped to bring peace and create stronger unity?
- Reflect together on the images Paul uses in 2:19-22: "fellow citizens," "members of God's household," and "a holy temple in the Lord." In what ways do you see each of these relating to unity in Christ? What other images help you to think of God's people as a unified whole?
- What does unity do for you as a part of God's people? What do your efforts at unity do for God?

Goalsetting (5 minutes)

Try working on the following goal as a result of this session:

- With the Spirit's help, I would like to work in the following ways so that I can help God's people grow in unity:

Closing (10-15 minutes)

Preparing for Prayer—Share items that you'd like the others in your group to bring to God in prayer for you. Feel free to mention praises, concerns, and goals that you've set so far in this study of Ephesians.

Prayer—Close with prayer, asking God to help all of you see the divisions and hostilities that need to be broken down so that believers in Christ can live and serve God in unity. Everyone may join in with prayer concerns and praises. As a reminder of Jesus' great work for us and God's amazing love for us all, you may also wish to read together Jesus' prayer for all believers from John 17:20-26.

Group Project (Optional)

As a group you may wish to commit to breaking down barriers in your church community and beyond in the name of Jesus, who came to make one new people—to the praise of God's glory. Ideas like these can help us work toward unity and welcome newcomers into God's family, the body of Christ.

- Begin a prayer group dedicated to praying for non-Christian neighbors and friends to come to the Lord.
- Be an advocate for persons with physical or cognitive impairments. Call Friendship Ministries at 1-888-866-8966 for information on teaching persons with cognitive impairments and enfolding them into the church.
- Work to promote literacy. Call Faith Alive at 1-800-333-8300 for information on creating a literacy program and working with persons who need to learn or grow in their reading skills.
- Work against the barriers of racism, abuse, poverty, and other social ills—not only in your personal life and church community but also in government and social structures in your wider community, state, and nation.
- Learn more about the Christian churches in your community and how they serve Christ in this world. Become familiar with their teachings and then get to know these churches

firsthand by visiting their worship services, meeting with pastors and other members, learning about their education and outreach ministries, and more—to build relationships in Jesus' name.

For example, you could use your common ground in Christ to coordinate ministry activities in your neighborhoods—such as vacation Bible school, mission-emphasis picnics, house of prayer ministries, food programs for needy people, thrift stores, financial planning and tax preparation, road or stream cleanup projects, house-building or remodeling projects, and more. Projects like this can develop into joint ministries that not only strengthen the church but also help change lives for eternity.

How does the mystery hidden for ages affect us as the church today?

EPHESIANS 3

5

Called to Serve and Grow—More Than We Imagine!

Ephesians 3

1For this reason I, Paul, the prisoner of Christ Jesus for the sake of you Gentiles—

2Surely you have heard about the administration of God's grace that was given to me for you, 3that is, the mystery made known to me by revelation, as I have already written briefly. 4In reading this, then, you will be able to understand my insight into the mystery of Christ, 5which was not made known to men in other generations as it has now been revealed by the Spirit to God's holy apostles and prophets. 6This mystery is that through the gospel the Gentiles are heirs together with Israel, members together of one body, and sharers together in the promise in Christ Jesus.

7I became a servant of this gospel by the gift of God's grace given me through the working of his power. 8Although I am less than the least of all God's people, this grace was given me: to preach to the Gentiles the unsearchable riches of Christ, 9and to make plain to everyone the administration of this mystery, which for ages past was kept hidden in God, who created all things. 10His intent was that now, through the church, the manifold wisdom of God should be made known to the rulers and authorities in the heavenly realms, 11according to his eternal purpose which he accomplished in Christ Jesus our Lord. 12In him and through faith in him we may approach God with freedom and confidence. 13I ask you, therefore, not to be discouraged because of my sufferings for you, which are your glory.

14For this reason I kneel before the Father, 15from whom his whole family in heaven and on earth derives its name. 16I pray that out of his glorious riches he may strengthen you with power through his Spirit in your inner being, 17so that Christ may dwell in your hearts through faith. And I pray that you, being rooted and established in love, 18may have power, together with all the saints, to grasp how wide and long and high and deep is the love of Christ, 19and to know this love that surpasses knowledge—that you may be filled to the measure of all the fullness of God.

20Now to him who is able to do immeasurably more than all we ask or imagine, according to his power that is at work within us, 21to him be glory in the church and in Christ Jesus throughout all generations, for ever and ever! Amen.

An Important Parenthesis

Just for fun, try diagramming some of Paul's sentences sometime. It can be a nightmare, especially when the sentence goes on and on, as in the original text for the twelve verses of Ephesians 3:2-13!

Paul stops his train of thought midway through his opening sentence in this section (3:1). Something important has come to mind, and he wishes to share it with his readers. The thought can't wait, so he sidelines the main sentence for a while. Verse 14 marks the place where Paul comes around to his earlier train of thought and then brings it to conclusion, ending at 3:21. But the material in between (3:2-13) is an important, purposeful parenthesis that reminds Paul's Gentile readers of a great mystery that "for ages past was kept hidden in God": their salvation through the finished work of Christ, who came to fulfill God's promises, break down barriers of hostility, and welcome believers from all nations into God's family.

Paul's Mission

Paul had a mission in life—an unflinching commitment to be a herald of Jesus Christ. He lived and breathed that mission. It got him going in the morning, and he dreamed about it at night. In Acts 20:24 Paul sums up his life charter this way:

> "I consider my life worth nothing to me, if only I may finish the race and complete the task the Lord Jesus has given me—the task of testifying to the gospel of God's grace."

Paul didn't think up this calling by himself. Rather, it was a charge laid on him, a "gift of God's grace" (3:7; see 3:2), and it gave him a crisp answer to life's central questions: *Who am I? Why am I here? Where am I going?* Simply stated, Paul was a servant of Jesus mandated "to preach to the Gentiles the unsearchable riches of Christ" (3:8). This mission would consume him for the rest of his days, and he gave to it his entire being.

Why all this activity and effort, often in the face of deep human and spiritual resistance and even threats to his life? Paul notes that he was entrusted by God himself with this task. Paul knew that from this strategic activity—as long as God willed it—nothing could tear him away.

Paul kept his head on straight and his priorities in order while he discharged his task. He kept reminding himself—and telling others—that he himself was no big deal. He called himself "less than the least" (3:8—the original word here has a comparative ending attached to a superlative, so it literally means "leaster" or "lessermost"). Paul was well aware of the ever-present danger of becoming a celebrity. Christians may well become famous—Paul himself became very well known—but they may never think of themselves as bigger and more significant than the task to which they have been called.

Paul ran from any hint of celebrity status. He makes this clear again to his readers in 3:13, saying that his sufferings are their "glory." In this way Paul comes back to his point in 3:1 and thus explains the reason for his parenthesis: to reassure his readers of his authenticity as a "prisoner of Christ Jesus for the sake of you Gentiles" (3:1). Paul knew, and he wanted his readers to know, that it was God's lavish favor—grace alone (3:2, 7-8; see 2:8-9)—that had turned him into a "man with a mission."

God's Grand Purpose

Through Paul's exalted words in 3:10-11 God's Spirit permits us a brief and powerful glimpse of what the Lord is doing through human history. The one almighty God is accomplishing his purposes day by day in Christ. This mighty work is not always visible in the external events of history. But by faith in God we can begin to look beneath the surface and see what is really happening there, and we can note with awe the God who is ceaselessly at work.

"Through the church" God is making his wisdom known "to the rulers and authorities in the heavenly realms" (3:10). Scholars debate over who these "rulers and authorities" are, but, as the "Additional Notes" on 3:10 point out, "it seems consistent with 1:21 and 6:12 to think of them as the hostile heavenly forces that stand opposed to the Lord. By this interpretation, the church stands as God's clear testimony to such powers concerning the divine plan of salvation." Always accomplishing his plans, God is guiding history home to its victorious end.

God is in charge, and because of Christ we are amazingly privileged to "approach God with freedom and confidence" (3:12). Therefore, says Paul, none who belong to Christ need ever lose heart or become "discouraged" (3:13).

What a picture Paul presents: we see a *big God* accomplishing *grand designs,* in part *through faithful heralds* who are *saved by grace* and *given the mission* to share *"the unsearchable riches of Christ"* (3:8). When we meditate on this picture, it can charge our courage and strengthen us each day with the compelling purpose of living for God in Christ by the power of the Holy Spirit.

How and to Whom Paul Prays

When we want to understand how much a Christian cares about other believers, one of the best ways to learn is by listening to the way that person prays for them. In Ephesians 3:14-21 Paul utters a sublime, affirming prayer for his beloved Christian brothers and sisters. Even Paul's posture for this prayer is significant. The apostle falls to his knees for a time of solemn pleading with God on behalf of his friends.

"For this reason I kneel" (3:14), says Paul. For what reason? Paul is referring to what he mentioned back in 2:19-22: his desire that his friends continue to be "built together to become a dwelling in which God lives by his Spirit." Paul longed for these believers to grow spiritually and become the temple, the body of Christ, from which God's glory would shine.

The way we view God when we pray shapes the very nature of how we pray and what we pray for. Paul addresses his plea to "the Father, from whom his whole family in heaven and on earth derives its name" (3:14-15). Paul, his Ephesian brothers and sisters, and every other group of Christians together comprise the family of God. Together we are children of the Father (4:6). We belong to God in Christ, and we begin to reflect the traits of God's character.

When we pray, then, we are not screaming for the attention of some distant, uncaring deity. We are praying to our "Father," the very One who made us, who continues to care about us and will never turn away from us in unconcern (see John 10:28-29; Heb. 13:5-6). God is delighted when we come to speak with him, especially when, as we see in Paul's example, we remember others within the family who are precious to God. Praying for his Christian friends here, Paul is confident that God hears his plea.

What Paul Prays For

Paul's central desire for his readers, his chief request to God for them, is that they may grow spiritually. To Paul, a people's relationship with God is more important than anything else: "I pray that out of his glorious riches he may strengthen you with power through his Spirit in your inner being" (3:16). God's "glorious riches" for blessing are infinite and breathtaking in their splendor. So Paul is not hesitant to make a huge request on behalf of his readers: that God will strengthen them with divine power.

To make a plea for power is to admit that we do not possess this power in ourselves. We human beings by ourselves are tired, fragile, and weak. So this is not about "giving it our best shot" or even "doing our personal best" to dedicate ourselves to God. Trying that, we'll fail every time. Our own power is pitifully limited.

Most people limp through life using the normal strength and power available to them. Every once in a while, though, they find themselves facing an obstacle that taxes their powers to the limit. Then they need extraordinary strength, a fresh and unusual burst of power from an outside unusual source. On their own power, people can do nothing to make the slightest spiritual progress. Sin acts as a brake upon them so that the engines of their heart are powerless to move their spiritual lives forward.

By depending daily on the presence and power of God's Spirit, however, believers can progress. Christ himself comes to "dwell"—literally, "to settle down in and take up residence"—ever more fully in their hearts (3:17). Receiving his regular supply of energy, believers in Jesus continue to advance toward the destination God has intended for them—to become patterned and shaped more and more by Jesus himself (see 2 Cor. 3:18). Jesus promises growth and strength to every believer who receives nourishment through the power of Christ's Spirit (John 15:5-8; Gal. 5:22-25).

Growing is not a quick, one-time event, of course. It's a lifelong process of day-by-day dwelling on and chewing the nourishing, power-transmitting promises and commands of God's Word. And along the way we discover that God, through his Spirit and Word, transfuses into us as much spiritual stamina and strength as we need to face our situations and overcome our circumstances.

Paul prays, too, that his readers, "being rooted and established in love, may have power, together with all the saints, to grasp how wide and long and high and deep is the love of Christ, and to know this love that surpasses knowledge" (3:17-19). Paul wants his readers to see that they are like flowers and leaves on a plant that continuously draws nourishment from its invisible roots. They are also "established" on a well-laid foundation (3:17). Christ's love, the solid foundation on which Christian living is set, is also the fountain from which that living flows in "power" (3:18). Paul also wants his readers to see that they are not alone. Of course, they enjoy unity with God in Christ through the Holy Spirit, but an added benefit is that they can "have power" to "grasp" the immense love of Christ "together with all the saints" who make up the body of Christ (3:18).

Further, Paul desires that they "know this love that surpasses knowledge" (3:19). This curious phrase points to more than head knowledge, more than grasping that Christ's love is in all and through all (3:18; see 4:6). Truly *knowing* Christ's love is possible only by experience, by the sort of personal, intimate knowledge shared by close friends—and yet is deeper still. Knowing Christ is the ultimate relationship possible for human beings, and it results in growth and newness of life—to the utmost. As Paul says, in knowing this love we "may be filled to the measure of all the fullness of God" (3:19).

How can we "know" the love of Christ? Through the Father's strengthening "with power through his Spirit in [our] inner being, so that Christ may dwell in [our] hearts through faith" (3:16-17). Only the efforts of the incomparably powerful Three-in-One can supply us, to the depths of our inner being, with the power "to know this love" (3:19). That's why Paul prays—because this love and the fullness it brings are only God's to give.

A Note of Boundless Praise

The size of your God governs the size of your faith. So, the bigger your God, the bigger your confidence in him—as well as the confidence of your prayers. The inverse, however, is not true. The size of your faith can't govern the size of your God. So never let yourself believe that anything is too big or too difficult for the one almighty God. God "is able to do immeasurably more than all we ask or imagine" (3:20).

In this phrase "immeasurably more" Paul piles one superlative about God on top of another. He makes one word out of three—*hyperekperissou* literally means "over and above, quite completely, more and beyond." Paul's praying was never limited by what he thought might be possible. He knew there was an immense store of riches and power available from God, a reservoir far bigger than he could ever imagine. And, best of all, it's available to "everyone who believes" (Rom. 1:16; see Eph. 3:21).

Paul ends this exalted prayer appropriately with an ascription of glory to God "in the church," "in Christ Jesus," and "throughout all generations"—and not just in history as we know it but "for ever and ever!" (3:21; see 1:4-6).

Additional Notes

3:9—The apostle refers to his commission "to make plain to everyone the administration of this mystery." The word he uses for "make plain" (*photizo,* from which our English word *photo* comes) means "to enlighten." Paul uses a form of the same word in 1:18 when he prays "that the eyes of your heart may be enlightened." The picture in 3:9 is that of bringing something to light—namely, the mystery of God's salvation for people of all nations, which was hidden for ages. Recall the words of Jesus when he first commissioned Paul: "I am sending you to [the Gentiles] to open their eyes and turn them from darkness to light" (Acts 26:17-18).

3:10—There is debate about the identity of "the rulers and authorities in the heavenly realms," to whom "the manifold wisdom of God" is made known "through the church." Some scholars believe Paul is referring to earthly governments and powers. John Stott sees this as a reference to the angels in heaven as "spectators of the drama of salvation" (*God's New Society*). But it seems more consistent with 1:21 and 6:12 to think of them as the hostile heavenly forces that stand opposed to the Lord. By this interpretation, the church stands as God's clear testimony to such powers concerning the divine plan of salvation.

3:20—Paul's rhetoric is stretched almost to the breaking point as he tries to describe God's infinite ability to deliver on our bold requests. Note the build-up of Paul's thought, according to commentator Andrew Lincoln:

> God is said to be able to do what believers ask in prayer; he is able to do what they might fail to ask but what they can think; he is able to do all (*panta*) they ask or think; he is able to do above all (*hyper panta*) they ask or think; he is able to do abundantly above all (*perissou hyper panta*) they ask or think; he is able to do more abundantly above all (*ekperissou hyper panta*) they ask or think; he is able to do infinitely more abundantly above all (*hyperekperissou hyper panta*) they ask or think. And what is more . . . this inexpressible power is at work within us!

GENERAL DISCUSSION

1. "Paul had a mission in life, an unflinching commitment to be a herald of Jesus Christ. . . . It got him going in the morning, and he dreamed about it at night." Do you feel a calling and desire to witness to the gospel as well? Do you observe it in your church? Why or why not? What have you learned from Ephesians 3 that might renew or reinforce a passion for witness in your personal life and in the life of your church?

2. Paul refers to himself as "less than the least of all God's people" (Eph. 3:8). What does this assessment tell us about Paul's priorities? How do you account for his saying this and yet feeling worthy of the calling to serve Christ?

3. In the light of Ephesians 3:6, 10-11, how would you respond to statements like these: "I can accept Christianity, but not the church" and "The church is the biggest obstacle to the spread of the gospel today."

4. What do our prayers say about our heart? What do our prayers say about the size of our God? What factors in our lives today might make it hard to "think big" in our prayer life?

5. Focusing on the requests Paul makes in Ephesians 3:16-19, comment on the statement "Paul's central desire for his readers . . . is that they may grow spiritually." In what ways do your fellow church members show their interest in growing spiritually together? In talking about their faith? In what ways might they (and you) do these things more clearly or effectively?

6. Paul prays that his readers "may have power, together with all the saints, to grasp how wide and long and high and deep is the love of Christ" (Eph. 3:18). Give one or two concrete examples of how one or more of the "saints" around you have enriched your grasp of the love of Christ, "who is able to do immeasurably more than all we ask or imagine" (3:20). What does this say about the importance of being an active part of the fellowship of God's people?

SMALL GROUP SESSION IDEAS

Opening (10-15 minutes)

Pray—Begin your meeting with prayer, asking for guidance as you discuss the revelation of God's good news and the mission of serving Christ and his church. Give thanks together for the opportunity to approach God in prayer through Christ and because of his saving work. Ask also that you may continue growing together in understanding and love.

Share—Share with each other how you're doing on goals set in previous lessons. You may also wish to share about your progress on group projects you may be doing.

Focus—Keep the following question in mind as you work through this session: *How important is the church to me, and how do I view its mission?*

Growing (35-40 minutes)

Read (Optional)—You may want to read together the Scripture passage for this lesson (along with the study guide notes) before moving into your discussion time.

Discuss—Choose from among the following process questions as you work through the General Discussion questions.

- What do you think of Paul's example as a servant of the gospel?
- What's the first example that comes to mind when you think of the church's failings? Share why this example is significant to you, if you feel comfortable doing so.

- As a group, list as many positive aspects of the church as you can think of. When the church has a positive impact, who would you say is responsible? Explain.
- Share your thoughts on how you can help build up the church in Christ's power through prayer, work, and fellowship.
- Share together some of your experiences of the wide, long, high, and deep love of Christ. In what ways have these experiences equipped you to share that love and build up the church as the body of Christ?
- In what ways have you seen God do more than you expected or imagined in your life? In the life of the church? In the communities and the wider world around you?

Goalsetting (5 minutes)

Try working on the following goal as you seek to live for Christ:

- With God's guidance and strength, I want to help the church work against its failings and grow as the body of Christ in the following ways:

Closing (10-15 minutes)

Preparing for Prayer—Share items that you'd like the others in your group to bring to God in prayer for you. Mention personal concerns and praises, goals you've set so far in this study, and so on.

Prayer—Close your meeting with prayer, asking the Spirit to empower each of you to serve Christ and his church faithfully and with awe at the amazing God who puts purpose in our lives and is guiding the course of history. Ask the Lord to give you the power, together with all believers, to understand and experience his love. Everyone may join in with prayer concerns and praises. You may also wish to include a reading of Jesus' prayer in John 17:20-26 to focus on unity, the topic of the next lesson.

Group Project (Optional)

As a group, compose your own prayer for your church, based on what you see as its main needs or challenges. You may also want to share this prayer with your church leaders and perhaps ask if your group might offer it as part of a congregational prayer during a worship service.

What makes the church attractive to people today?

6

EPHESIANS 4:1-16

Unity Toward Maturity

Ephesians 4:1-16

1As a prisoner for the Lord, then, I urge you to live a life worthy of the calling you have received. 2Be completely humble and gentle; be patient, bearing with one another in love. 3Make every effort to keep the unity of the Spirit through the bond of peace. 4There is one body and one Spirit—just as you were called to one hope when you were called—5one Lord, one faith, one baptism; 6one God and Father of all, who is over all and through all and in all.

7But to each one of us grace has been given as Christ apportioned it. 8This is why it says:

> "When he ascended on high,
> he led captives in his train
> and gave gifts to men."

9(What does "he ascended" mean except that he also descended to the lower, earthly regions? 10He who descended is the very one who ascended higher than all the heavens, in order to fill the whole universe.)

11It was he who gave some to be apostles, some to be prophets, some to be evangelists, and some to be pastors and teachers, 12to prepare God's people for works of service, so that the body of Christ may be built up 13until we all reach unity in the faith and in the knowledge of the Son of God and become mature, attaining to the whole measure of the fullness of Christ.

14Then we will no longer be infants, tossed back and forth by the waves, and blown here and there by every wind of teaching and by the cunning and craftiness of men in their deceitful scheming. 15Instead, speaking the truth in love, we will in all things grow up into him who is the Head, that is, Christ. 16From him the whole body, joined and held together by every supporting ligament, grows and builds itself up in love, as each part does its work.

Two Central Truths

The core of the biblical message is not what people have been able to do for God, but rather *who God is* and *what God has done for them.*

Who is God? Jewish children, even before learning their own name, were taught to say this text: "Hear, O Israel, the LORD our God, the LORD is one" (Deut. 6:4). It states one of the most compelling and important realities of life. Every Jew repeated these powerful words every day throughout his or her life as a central confession of faith.

What has God done? God has created a people, chosen them, loved them, and rescued them. As their Father in Christ, God is now pleased to call them his children. God carries them for the rest of their days, sustains them moment by moment, and promises to bring them home. Having done everything for his people, God is "over all and through all and in all." There is, therefore, "one God and Father of all" (Eph. 4:6).

From these two central truths everything else in the Bible follows—including how God's people are to live in response. In the first half of his letter to the Ephesians Paul has presented what the one true God has done for his people. In the second half Paul lays out for his fellow believers the implications of these core teachings for their life together. Who they are—God's own people—must give shape to what they do. Their identity must shape their obedience.

Note again that good doctrine (right thinking about God and his ways with his people) is vital to good ethics (right teachings about how to live). Christian doctrine that does not result in Christian ethics is sterile and incomplete; ethics without doctrine lacks foundation and becomes directionless and incoherent.

Live Worthily—Keep Unity

As the church, the body of Christ, we need to guard against becoming polarized. Our conversation and manners toward one another can easily grow coarse. Sometimes churches and their members do more shouting at one another than talking and discussing. Sometimes believers arm themselves with arguments to get their point across. Too often the results have been distressing splits within God's family. Some people, it seems, prefer winning an argument to loving their brother or sister in Christ. John Henry Newman once said, "Oh, how we hate one another for the love of Christ."

God weeps when we argue and fight with one another because, belonging to the "one God and Father of all" (4:6), we also belong to one another. And any form of hate—belittling or insulting by thoughts, words, looks, or gestures (see Heidelberg Catechism Q&A 105)—is murder and thus a violation of one of God's central commands (Matt. 5:21-22).

Moved by God's Spirit, Paul pleads with his readers—and with us too: "Make every effort to keep the unity of the Spirit through the bond of peace" (4:3).

Paul issues this appeal from his position as a "prisoner for the Lord" (4:1). He has said it before (3:1), and he must say it again, for he knows that all he is and everything he does must flow from his identity in Christ. More and more, Paul is taking on the character qualities of his Lord. He can go only where Christ wants him to go, led by the Holy Spirit. Never, therefore, can he chart his course by the whims of public opinion. His Lord's desires are Paul's commands. And in the Spirit they are Paul's desires too.

Paul "urges" his readers (4:1). The Greek verb for "urge" (*parakaleo*) means "to summon to one's side, to call for help." To Paul, maintaining unity among believers for Christ's sake was not a take-it-or-leave-it option. To live in unity and harmony together is the Lord's command, and to do so takes strong, deliberate, daily effort. Fully aware of how difficult the task really is, Paul begs; he issues a strong summons and appeal for the sake of God's honor.

Christians are "to live a life worthy" of their calling (4:1). The word for "worthy" here (*axios*) originally meant "bringing up the other beam of the scales, bringing into balance." In other words, the one side of their lives, *being* children of God and sharing in all the privileges of that position, must have a corresponding counterbalance—namely, *living* as children of God. The "calling [they] have received" (4:1) comes from the sovereign Lord of history.

Features of a Worthy Life

Paul lists five specific features of a life "worthy of the calling" we have received (4:1). He begins with "Be completely humble" (4:2). The word for "humble" here (*tapeinophrosyne*) means "considering or weighing with a lowly spirit." In the surrounding culture of the Greeks, humility was anything but a virtue. Greeks were passionate about prominence, self-importance, and distinction. To them, humility, the distinguishing mark among Christ's followers, was a sad, deplorable character flaw found in those who "just couldn't make it" in life. Never—not in their wildest thinking—could the Greeks imagine humility as a character trait to be desired. Nor can many of us today.

However strongly we may hear the siren call to become great and make a name for ourselves, either outside the Christian fellowship or within it, we Christians must remember that in our Lord's kingdom the way down is up. And the way up, unmistakably, is down (see Phil. 2:5-13).

Next Paul advises his readers to be "gentle" (*prautes*—4:2). Sometimes translated as "meek," the word does not mean "wishy-washy" or "wimpy." Rather, it means that even in the face of adversity, Christians are strong and yet gentle in their response—controlled, not belligerent, measured, peaceable through and through. Only those who know they belong wholly to God can be truly gentle, of course, for they are convinced that they need not take things into their own hands and clobber their opponents when things go against them. God will care for them, so they can be quiet—gentle in their heart and actions.

God's followers must also be "patient" (4:2). The Greek word here (*makrothumia*) means, literally, "steadfast, even-tempered, forbearing." Knowing that God is in control of their lives, believers need not—must not—insist on instantaneous results or a fast-paced response. Christians are to be patient with each other—"with everyone," in fact (1 Thess. 5:14). The Greeks had little regard for this virtue also. It was far better, they advised, to strike back—immediately—when circumstances wouldn't budge or people didn't cooperate.

The fourth feature of a worthy Christian life is "bearing with one another in love" (4:2). Haters increase tensions. Frustration, resentment, and anger can never be stopped unless cut off from the evil air in which they thrive. The best, most potent—and most Christlike—defense against one's enemies is to take their evil assaults and, bearing with these persons in selfless love (*agape*), render those assaults impotent. The apostle Peter taught that expressing such love "covers over a multitude of sins" (1 Pet. 4:8).

Finally, Christians are "to make every effort to keep the unity of the Spirit through the bond of peace" (Eph. 4:3). The original word for "make every effort" (*spoudazo*) means "to make haste, to be intent and diligent, eager." So our deliberate aim as Christians must ever be to eagerly maintain unity and peace among ourselves.

Notice also that this unity is not some smooth (or rickety) strategy put together by human ingenuity and goodwill. It's the "unity of the Spirit," a gift from God to be treasured by us in faith. We *are* in fact united in God through the Spirit's presence and power among us; so we are to cherish and maintain this unity by walking in a manner worthy of our calling to be God's children. Doing so, we shall be showing the world what it means to belong together in Christ.

Jesus' Urgent Plea

In his high-priestly prayer Jesus pleaded with his Father, "I pray . . . that all of them may be one, Father, just as you are in me and I am in you. . . . May they be brought to complete unity to let the world know that you sent me and have loved them even as you have loved me" (John 17:20-23).

Peace and unity among his followers matters a lot to Jesus. These features of a worthy life should therefore also matter to us. But we're not left to work at these things on our own. Jesus also prayed, "Father, I want those you have given me to be with me where I am" (John 17:24), and "when he ascended," as Ephesians 4:8 puts it, "he led captives in his train and gave gifts to men." Using language here that reflects the practice of earthly conquerors, Paul is saying not only that we have a place promised for us in Christ's presence for eternity (John 14:2-3) but also that we have gifts of grace we may use now to help us grow closer to God and to one another.

A Gift for Every Member

Christ calls and equips members of his body, and he sovereignly determines how his gifts are distributed among them. There's no room for triumphalistic or—at the other extreme—"I'm-not-worth-anything" attitudes on our part. The fellowship suffers if a person fails to use his or her gifts or if others despise or demean a gift a person has been given. No matter what they do—choir members, church school teachers, elders, deacons, sound technicians, hospitality servants, preachers, nursery attendants—all are equipped by Christ for their task and placed by divine appointment.

Though the list of gifts in Ephesians 4 is not exhaustive (see also Rom. 12:4-8; 1 Cor. 12:7-11, 27-30), Paul mentions five positions within the fellowship: apostles, prophets, evangelists, pastors, and teachers.

Apostles—the Greek word *apostolos* means "sent one, delegated to discharge a mission." Jesus called his original twelve apostles so that "they might be with him and that he might send them out to preach and to have authority to drive out demons" (Mark 3:14-15). In other words, they were to learn from Jesus about the kingdom of God and to proclaim it. Witnesses of the risen Lord, the apostles laid the foundation of the church (1 Cor. 12:28; Eph. 2:20).

Prophets too were vitally important to the founding of the church (1 Cor. 12:28; Eph. 2:20). Like their Old Testament counterparts, the prophets in the New Testament church clarified for believers what God was doing in the times they lived in. But there were false prophets as well as true ones (1 John 4:1), so the Christian fellowship always had to be alert to their messages and discern whether they were speaking a word from the Lord. In a sense, all followers of Jesus have a prophetic calling to bring God's Word into their everyday life and surroundings.

Evangelists are mentioned only a few times in the New Testament (see also Acts 21:8; 2 Tim. 4:5). As they proclaimed and promoted the good news of Jesus, they were the church's first missionaries. Their vocation, "to evangelize" (*evangelizo*), is mentioned fifty-four times in the New Testament, and the "gospel" (*evangelion*) they proclaimed is mentioned seventy-six times. Unbelievers matter to God. The Lord's evangelists were and still are God's strategic voice in calling unbelievers into the fellowship of the forgiven.

Pastors and teachers (poimenas kai didaskalos). The original words here imply shepherding and instruction for the Lord's flock. As people left the darkness of unbelief and sin and entered the light of God's hope and righteousness, it was the pastors' and teachers' important responsibility to build these persons up and help them grow spiritually, teaching them and giving them spiritual guidance and care.

Toward Spiritual Maturity

God has a specific purpose in giving us gifts: "so that the body of Christ may be built up until we all reach unity in the faith and . . . become mature, attaining to the whole measure of the fullness of Christ" (4:12-13). Without gifts, believers would remain "infants, tossed back and forth by the waves, and blown here and there by every wind of teaching" (4:14).

The deepest longing God has for the church is to help believers become all they're meant to be in Jesus—to attain "the fullness of Christ" (4:13). By the time a believer dies and departs the earthly body of Christ, he or she ought to look a lot more like Jesus. Never, therefore, can the church remain static, unchanging. It ought *always* to be changing—growing toward what God intends.

All other purposes for God's church—evangelism, relief of the world's social distress, moral influence upon a wicked society, providing safe haven from the world's evil, and so on—flow out of God's foundational purpose to grow "all" believers into spiritually mature daughters and sons (4:13).

Unity, Truth, Love

Christians must become more and more unified. In 4:2 Paul encouraged his readers to keep unity in the Spirit and to be bound together in peace. Here he calls for two additional dimensions of that unity. We must reach "unity in the faith and in the knowledge of the Son of God" (4:13). More and more, God's people must come to know—with their heads and in their hearts—the unsearchable depths of God's love for them expressed in Christ (Rom. 11:33-36; Eph. 3:17-19) and of the power of Christ's resurrection within them (Phil. 3:10). Together believers must study God's truth more and more, growing to trust God more and more. Doing so, they will inevitably grow in the unity God intends.

As Christians learn to "[speak] the truth in love" (4:15), they grow into spiritual adulthood. No longer are they like infants—ignorant, vacillating, interested in one thing at one moment and in another thing at the next. Rather, they will have stability and rootedness (3:17). They will not fall prey to every whim and fad that comes along.

Finally, unity and truth must be permeated by love within the Christian fellowship. Without love, unity and truth are sterile. What good is it, lacking love, to be unified in grim duty? What good is it, lacking love, to be impeccably—and acridly—orthodox? Further, telling the truth without love can be divisive, bringing disunity. Love freshens the body of Christ, keeps the unity among its members vibrant and bright, and produces a truth-telling that is fragrant, full, and wonderfully nourishing. (See 1 Cor. 13.)

A Lifelong Process

Spiritual growth is not a momentary event. It's a lifelong process. As the Heidelberg Catechism indicates, "In this life even the holiest have only a small beginning of [perfect] obedience. Nevertheless, with all seriousness of purpose, they do begin to live according to all, not only some, of God's commandments" (Q&A 114).

Depending together on God, believers also need one another's help. That's why Paul speaks of "the whole body, joined and held together by every supporting ligament, grow[ing] and build[ing] itself up in love, as each part does its work" (4:16).

Oh, for the body of Christ to function as God intends! If it did, people would throng en masse to be a part of it. It would be so attractive to wandering and lost people that they would discover, perhaps for the first time, what life is really all about.

Additional Notes

4:1—"To live a life" is a translation of the Greek word for "walk." Paul uses the same word in Ephesians 2:2 (for "used to live") and in 2:10 (for "to do"). Behind the idea of "calling" lies the conviction that God's sovereign, gracious leading requires a continued human response of obedience.

4:16—Notice Paul's use of body imagery. He uses similar imagery in his discussion of spiritual gifts in Romans 12 and 1 Corinthians 12. There he emphasizes the interdependence of the body's members. Here in Ephesians Paul emphasizes the need for the members to grow together. The whole body must be active in growing and maturing together.

GENERAL DISCUSSION

1. Before discussing Ephesians 4, pause to reflect together on chapters 1-3. What have you learned from those chapters that motivates you to want to live a life of new obedience before the Lord?

2. Look again at the first two paragraphs in the preceding section "Live Worthily—Keep Unity." How do you respond to the observations there? From the perspective of Ephesians 4:3-6, how would you grade your church on the issue of unity? Your denomination? The worldwide church of Christ? What barriers to unity do you see at each of these church levels?

3. On the basis of Ephesians 4:1-6, what (more) can you do to promote unity that honors God? What (more) can your church do?

4. Why has Christ "apportioned" his gifts of grace rather than giving everyone all the gifts? What does Christ's giving of various gifts have to do with unity?

5. In the light of Ephesians 4:15-16, how do you respond to this statement: "One of the greatest attractions to Christianity is the church. Many people are attracted to community even before they are attracted to Christ"?

6. In Ephesians 4:15 Paul mentions "speaking the truth in love." What happens in the church when we are long on truth and short on love? How about when the opposite happens? Why is it important to maintain both truth and love? How do these help the church grow toward maturity?

SMALL GROUP SESSION IDEAS

Opening (10-15 minutes)

Pray/Worship—Open with prayer and a brief time of worship, celebrating what God has done for us all in Jesus Christ. Pray that each of you may experience the stirring of the Spirit to live wholly for Christ, as you focus together on unity in the church, Christ's body.

Share—Share with each other how you're doing on goals from previous lessons and on group projects you may have begun.

Focus—Consider the following question as you work through this session: *How much am I concerned about unity in the church?*

Growing (35-40 minutes)

Read (Optional)—You may want to read together the Scripture passage for this lesson. If there's time, you may also wish to read or review the study guide notes before moving into your discussion time.

Discuss—Choose from among the following process questions as you work through the General Discussion questions.

- General Discussion question 2 asks about barriers to unity that you've observed in the church at various levels. What barriers to unity do you see in your own life? In your small group? (Ask for the Spirit's guidance to help everyone participate in building up through love rather than tearing down.)
- Give an example or two of how Christ's gift of a leader in ministry helped to build up your church. In what ways did this build you up personally?
- How would you "speak the truth in love" to a church member who said, "I get so upset about people who call themselves Christians but don't do a thing for the church. On any Sunday I can look down my pew and see that most of the people sitting there are not spiritually mature."

Goalsetting (5 minutes)
Try working on the following goal in the coming week:

- Here's how I want to apply what I've learned about gifts, unity, and maturity in this lesson:

Closing (10-15 minutes)

Preparing for Prayer—Share items that you'd like others to bring to God in prayer.

Prayer—Close your meeting with prayer, asking the Lord to help you persevere in living "a life worthy of the calling" of being God's children (Eph. 4:1) as you seek to grow together in Christlike love and unity. Ask for guidance in learning about and using the gifts Christ has given you for the upbuilding and healing of his body, the church. Everyone may join in with personal prayer concerns and praises. If you like, close with a song such as "We Are One in the Spirit." Before leaving, you might also wish each other the peace of the Holy Spirit in the coming week.

Group Project/Study Goal (Optional)
Some or all of you may wish to learn more about spiritual gifts and how to use them in living for Christ as part of his church

today. Your pastor or education leader may be able to schedule a workshop for you and others to attend. Several excellent studies on spiritual gifts are available, including the revised *Discover Your Gifts and Learn How to Use Them* published by Faith Alive Christian Resources. Call 1-800-333-8300 or visit www.FaithAliveResources.org for more information.

Now that we are saved, we must remember who we are.

7

EPHESIANS 4:17-5:21

Children of Darkness, Children of Light

Ephesians 4:17-32

17So I tell you this, and insist on it in the Lord, that you must no longer live as the Gentiles do, in the futility of their thinking. 18They are darkened in their understanding and separated from the life of God because of the ignorance that is in them due to the hardening of their hearts. 19Having lost all sensitivity, they have given themselves over to sensuality so as to indulge in every kind of impurity, with a continual lust for more.

20You, however, did not come to know Christ that way. 21Surely you heard of him and were taught in him in accordance with the truth that is in Jesus. 22You were taught, with regard to your former way of life, to put off your old self, which is being corrupted by its deceitful desires; 23to be made new in the attitude of your minds; 24and to put on the new self, created to be like God in true righteousness and holiness.

25Therefore each of you must put off falsehood and speak truthfully to his neighbor, for we are all members of one body. 26"In your anger do not sin": Do not let the sun go down while you are still angry, 27and do not give the devil a foothold. 28He who has been stealing must steal no longer, but must work, doing something useful with his own hands, that he may have something to share with those in need.

29Do not let any unwholesome talk come out of your mouths, but only what is helpful for building others up according to their needs, that it may benefit those who listen. 30And do not grieve the Holy Spirit of God, with whom you were sealed for the day of redemption. 31Get rid of all bitterness, rage and anger, brawling and slander, along with every form of malice. 32Be kind and compassionate to one another, forgiving each other, just as in Christ God forgave you.

5:1-21

1Be imitators of God, therefore, as dearly loved children 2and live a life of love, just as Christ loved us and gave himself up for us as a fragrant offering and sacrifice to God.

3But among you there must not be even a hint of sexual immorality, or of any kind of impurity, or of greed, because these are improper for God's holy people. 4Nor should there be obscenity, foolish talk or coarse joking, which are out of place, but rather thanksgiving. 5For of this you can be sure: No immoral, impure or greedy person—such a man is an idolater—has any inheritance in the kingdom of Christ and of God. 6Let no one deceive you with empty words, for because of such things God's wrath comes on those who are disobedient. 7Therefore do not be partners with them.

8For you were once darkness, but now you are light in the Lord. Live as children of light 9(for the fruit of the light consists in all goodness, righteousness and truth) 10and find out what pleases the Lord. 11Have nothing to do with the fruitless deeds of darkness, but rather expose them. 12For it is shameful even to mention what the disobedient do in secret. 13But everything exposed by the light becomes visible, 14for it is light that makes everything visible. This is why it is said:

"Wake up, O sleeper,
rise from the dead,
and Christ will shine on you."

15Be very careful, then, how you live—not as unwise but as wise, 16making the most of every opportunity, because the days are evil. 17Therefore do not be foolish, but understand what the Lord's will is. 18Do not get drunk on wine, which leads to debauchery. Instead, be filled with the Spirit. 19Speak to one another with psalms, hymns and spiritual songs. Sing and make music in your heart to the Lord, 20always giving thanks to God the Father for everything, in the name of our Lord Jesus Christ.

21Submit to one another out of reverence for Christ.

No Longer!

In Ephesians 4:17-32 Paul calls the Ephesian Christians to leave their former way of life and to live as the people they have now become in the power of Christ. The apostle begins his appeal with "So" (literally, "Therefore"). In view of all that God has done for them (4:7-16), Paul insists on it "in the Lord" that believers must now "no longer live as the Gentiles do" (4:17). These Gentile unbelievers, Paul explains, are groping about in darkness. They are far from the life available in God (*apellotriomenoi* means "having been alienated," or "enemy-like"). Unbelief and evil are never neutral: they are aggressively pitted against God and resistant to new life in the Lord.

This opposition issues from "the ignorance that is in them due to the hardening of their hearts" (4:18). Sometimes ignorance is bliss; often it is innocent. In the case of these unbelievers, however, ignorance resulted from perverse hard-heartedness. These people could have—should have—known better than to act in unbelief as they did. For God had revealed himself to everyone (Rom. 1:18-25). In callous disregard they determined to squelch what they knew and to disobey God.

In the Bible "hardness of heart" means an attitude of persistent and blatant disregard of God and his ways. These unbelievers have continued to ignore and resist God for so long that they are now totally unable to do anything else. Their hearts are stone-hard, "having lost all sensitivity" (4:19).

The New Self in Christ

"You, however . . ."—Paul emphatically contrasts the "former way of life" (4:22) with the new life of believers in Christ. Not only have believers "heard of" Christ and been "taught in him" (4:21; literally, "learned from him"), they have "put off" the old self (4:22; see Rom. 6:6; Col. 3:9) and "put on the new self" (4:24). This is the metaphor for the process of daily conversion. Believers in Christ have left behind a pattern of living that was "corrupted"—ruined, rotten, spoiled—by perverse desires (4:22) and have put on a life fresh and bright, thoroughly renewed.

Renewal, as God intends it, is not some superficial discarding of a few bad traits. Renewal is a total, pervasive cutting out of the rotten core, a surgery so deep that one becomes a new person in the process. The overhaul begins with a decisive first step—the verbs for "put off" and "put on" indicate deliberate action—and the process continues with daily taking that step again and again. "To be made new in the attitude of [our] minds" (4:23) reveals how we can put off the old and put on the new—our way of thinking, our mind, gets a thorough scrubbing from God. The result is a person who has returned to the way he or she is supposed to be: "created to be like God in true righteousness and holiness" (4:24). Note also the use of verbs here: God does the work as we cooperate with him; we cannot even begin to put off the old self without the power of almighty God.

Putting the New Life into Practice

Paul next gets specific in prescribing patterns of life that help believers put off the old self and put on the new. His first appeal is this: "You must put off falsehood and speak truthfully" (4:25). In both the Old and New Testaments (see Ex. 20:16; Ps. 12; Matt. 5:33-37; 2 Cor. 2:17), God continually warns against pretense and artificiality. God hates any hint of saying one thing while meaning another, of acting one way while thinking another. Deceit is a pattern of activity that indicates one is not living by the fresh principles of Christ. Our Lord calls for authenticity. Among the fellowship of God's people, truthfulness must hold sway, for "we are all members of one body" (Eph. 4:25).

Second, believers are to deal with their anger (4:26-27). The anger Paul mentions here (*parorgismos*) is no momentary hotheadedness, a brief spilling over of turbulent emotions. Rather, it's a focused, relentless, determined, driven anger, powered by the deep energy of hate that can feed upon one's spirit and eventually consume a person. Such anger is vindictive. The only countermeasure to its terrible power is to deal with it quickly and regularly—every day before nightfall, in fact, so its ugliness won't carry over into the next day.

Third, stealing must surrender to sharing (4:28). Before their conversion, Paul's friends in Ephesus participated in all kinds of low-life practices, including cheating and swindling others; sometimes they violently robbed. "It's got to stop," says Paul, in effect; "replace your selfish, swindling practices by doing 'something good'—something honest and generous. Work for what you get, so that you may share with those in need." (For an amazingly current application of Paul's command here, see Heidelberg Catechism Q&A 110-111.) Paul himself lived by his own advice. Wherever he went on his missionary journeys, Paul worked for his food so as "not to be a burden to anyone" (1 Thess. 2:9; see 2 Thess. 3:6-15).

Fourth, Paul counsels his Ephesian friends to stop their gush of rotten words (*sapros* means "corrupt, foul, unwholesome, spoiled"—4:29). This is the only time this vivid adjective is used in the New Testament to describe something other than decomposed fruit, vegetables, fish, trees, and so on. Christians need to rid their vocabulary of what we call "coarse words," "foul speech," "gutter language" (see also 5:4)—and yet Paul means much more. Some words, however good or harmless in themselves, can be spoken at the wrong time or expressed in the wrong way to wound and even kill a person's spirit. Hence the clear warning of Heidelberg Catechism Q&A 105: "I am not to belittle, insult, hate, or kill my neighbor—not by my thoughts, my words, my look or gesture. . . ." (See also Rom. 12:17-21.)

Again Paul advises replacing an evil practice with a good one: speak "only what is helpful for building others up according to their needs, that it may benefit those who listen" (4:29). Graciousness ought to mark the speech of every person maturing in Christ. As Proverbs 25:11 says, "A word aptly spoken is like apples of gold in settings of silver."

Fifth, Paul warns his readers to "get rid of all bitterness, rage and anger, brawling and slander, along with every form of malice" (4:31)—a motley mass of ugliness proceeding from a mean, vengeful spirit. God's people must become "kind and compassionate to one another, forgiving each other." To do so is only fitting, for that's how God has treated them: "in Christ God forgave you" (4:32).

Who We Are

As Paul calls his readers to live with integrity in Christ, he reminds them of who they are: God's "dearly loved children" (5:1). Believers are neither orphans nor outcasts; they are part of the divine family. God, through Christ, has become their heavenly Father. And in much the same way that earthly children imitate their parents, these heavenly sons and daughters—and we—are to imitate God (5:1). Jesus challenged his disciples to the same standard as he spoke about loving their enemies: "Be perfect . . . as your heavenly Father is perfect" (Matt. 5:48).

In connection with this we are called to "live a life of love" (Eph. 5:2). The actual verb Paul uses is "to walk in love," a favorite metaphor for advancing and making progress in the Christian way. Of course, there are lots of ways in which we, simply because we are human (and sinfully so), cannot imitate God. But we *can* love, even as God loves us.

The greatest evidence of this divine love for us is that "Christ loved us and gave himself up for us as a fragrant offering and sacrifice to God" (5:2). In light of this, only one response is fitting: day by day our conduct must become more consistent with who we are. The verses that follow (5:3-18) set forth the deep contrasts between what it means to be "children of light" rather than of "darkness" (5:8), between those who are awake and those who are asleep (5:14), between those who are "wise" and those who are "foolish" (5:15, 17). As a result, these verses summarize what it means to put off the old self and put on the new (4:22-23).

Not Even a Hint

Paul's warning is bracing and direct: "Among you there must not be even a hint of sexual immorality, or of any kind of impurity, or of greed, because these are improper for God's holy people" (5:3). The original word for "sexual immorality" here is *porneia,* meaning "fornication." What a mighty revolution the first Christians introduced into the prevailing sexual ethic of their day. While among the Greeks it was considered inappropriate for women to have sexual relations with anyone but their husbands, men were allowed extramarital relations. Christianity, however, made clear that no one was to have sexual relations with anyone but his or her spouse.

Further, even "any kind of impurity" (*akatharsia pasa*) was to be avoided. This referred to behaviors that can incite unchastity and adultery, such as "actions, looks, talk, thoughts, or desires" (Heidelberg Catechism, Q&A 109)—a prudent warning for a society (not unlike ours) glutted with every imaginable kind of sexual expression.

Paul also sternly cautions any who might be tempted toward "obscenity, foolish talk or coarse joking" (5:4). Paul's word for "coarse joking" (*eutrapelia*) refers to base, perverted jesting—filthy talk. God's people ought never to participate in such depraved activity, no matter where they are or what they're doing—even if they're "just out with the boys" or if it's "girls' night out."

Perverse talk, in whatever circumstances it takes place, is never harmless or excusable. It hurts—always. Actions have consequences. Evildoers invite "God's wrath" (*orge*—5:6). People can take sin too seriously, supposing that wrongdoing can never be forgiven. But people can also take sin not seriously enough, belittling the fact that it is a grievous affront to a holy and just God. Make no mistake, Paul explains—God will deal justly with "those who are disobedient" (5:6).

Living Fully and Well

Having warned his friends about what to avoid, Paul also points out what they should embrace. "Thanksgiving" must replace obscenity, foolish talk, and coarse joking (5:4). Life itself is a gift. To use it properly means celebrating and enjoying the gift itself while giving thanks to the Giver (5:20). We might even whistle or sing a song, making "music in [our hearts] to the Lord" (5:19).

In Christ we can live like the old Puritan whose epitaph says it all: "He lived until he died." Longing to know God in every situation and striving to do his will in every moment the Lord graciously provides—this is what Paul means by "making the most of every opportunity" (literally, "redeeming the time"—5:16). We are to live fully and well, no matter how short or long our lives are.

But how can we not only determine to be "wise" (5:15) but also carry it out in practice? Our minds are so weak and tired, and our wills are weaker still. By ourselves we simply *cannot* do as we should, even if we want to (Rom. 7:14-25; Gal. 5:17).

Two things are important. First, we must rely daily on God, declaring again and again our dependence on him "for everything" (5:20). We really need God's presence and extraordinary power; we need to be "filled with the Spirit" (5:18). Thus, says Paul, everything we do must be done "in the name of our Lord Jesus Christ" (5:20).

Second, a fellow-battler can help—immensely. She or he can serve as a spiritual accountability partner, someone who is on our side in our furious struggle with evil. About such a relationship of mutual accountability Paul says, "Submit to one another out of reverence for Christ" (5:21). Accountability partners can pray for each other, help each other remain honest and authentic, and spot areas in each other's lives where they are especially vulnerable.

Careful Inspection

As we take an honest look at who we are and how we live, Paul urges us to depend on God, resolving each day to live as the Lord commands. It is wise, then, to

- know how powerful evil really is, and how weak we are in our efforts to resist it.
- understand that not every area of temptation is equally alluring. We have to be honest and clear about the areas where we're especially vulnerable.
- understand how temptation works: seeing leads to imagining, imagining to doing, doing to habits, and habits to character (see Matt. 18:8-9).
- develop a spiritual companionship—an accountability relationship—with at least one other person. That person can become a messenger ("angel") of God, helping us to resist evil.
- pray regularly for the Spirit's presence and power.

In his *Imitation of Christ*, Thomas à Kempis said, "Every day we ought to renew our purpose and refresh ourselves as though it were the first day of our conversion."

Additional Notes

5:2—What a striking contrast between the self-giving of Christ's love and the way of unbelievers in 4:19, who "have given themselves over to sensuality"!

5:6—The possibility of being deceived in the Ephesian context was very real, since "the Gnostics were arguing that bodily sins could be committed without damage to the soul, and with impunity" (John Stott, *God's New Society*).

5:7—When Paul warns against being "partners with" the disobedient, he uses a word (*symmetochos*) that connotes an intimate involvement or participation with others. He is not warning against all association with them.

GENERAL DISCUSSION

1. As Paul begins his appeal for a distinctive Christian lifestyle, what basis or motivation does he have in mind?

2. In practical terms, what does it mean to you to put off the old self and put on the new? What makes the daily process of "putting off" and "putting on" difficult?

3. In Ephesians 4:25-32 Paul specifies several practical ways for his readers to put off the old and put on the new. Review these together and comment on the relevance of each one for Christian living today.

4. In the light of Ephesians 5:1-2, how would you respond to this opinion: "If we really want the world to see that we are God's family, we have to be more bold to stand up for what is right. We have to stop sidestepping the problem of sin and start telling it like it is!"

5. What evidence do you see in our society and everyday living that we must continually battle all kinds of impurity? Are the many warnings in Ephesians 5 even making a difference in our culture? In our personal lives? Why does Paul add that these evils should be replaced with thankfulness? How can we, as "children of light," expose "the fruitless deeds of darkness" in ways that reveal the love of Christ?

6. What does it mean to "be filled with the Spirit" (Eph. 5:18)?

SMALL GROUP SESSION IDEAS

Opening (5-10 minutes)

Pray—Open with prayer, asking God to help you learn and grow as you focus on living a life that's pleasing to God in Christ, who "loved us and gave himself up for us" (Eph. 5:2).

Share—Share with each other how you're doing on your goals from previous lessons, and take this time to report on any group projects you may be doing. *Note:* This lesson about leaving the old life of sin and living for Jesus will fit in well with a brief discussion of the book *Not the Way It's Supposed to Be* (see group study project, lesson 3).

Focus—As you work through this session, try to keep the following in mind: *In what ways does my living for Christ make a difference in this world? In the lives of people around me?*

Growing (35-50 minutes)

Read (Optional)—You may want to read together the Scripture passage for this lesson (along with the study guide notes) before moving into your discussion time.

Discuss—Choose from among the following process questions as you work through the General Discussion questions.

- What motivates you to put off the old way of life and to keep it behind you?
- In your living for Christ, give one or two examples of how you try to be "in the world but not of it." When you've slipped up and had to ask forgiveness and try again, what lessons have you learned?
- In this lesson what have you learned about imitating God? About thankfulness? About being filled with the Spirit?
- Describe, if you wish, one or two experiences in which the Spirit's power has helped you in your living for Christ.

Goalsetting (5 minutes)

Try working on one of the following goals in the coming week:

- I want to dedicate (or rededicate) myself to living distinctively for Christ. I need to work on these areas of my life, in the Spirit's power:

- Here's how I want to apply what I've learned in this lesson about living for Christ:

Closing (5-10 minutes)

Preparing for Prayer—Share items that you'd like the others in your group to bring to God in prayer for you.

Prayer—Close with prayer, thanking God for providing a way for us to put off our old selves and put on our new selves in Christ. Ask God to give each of you a special measure of grace as you try to "live a life of love" for Jesus' sake (5:2). Everyone may join in with prayer concerns and praises. Encourage each other to "be filled with the Spirit" and, if you like, choose a favorite song or two with which you can "speak to one another" and "make music in your heart to the Lord" (5:19).

Transformation in Christ carries over into all our relationships.

8

EPHESIANS 5:21-6:9

Marriage, Families, and Workers in Christ

Ephesians 5:21-33

21 Submit to one another out of reverence for Christ.

22 Wives, submit to your husbands as to the Lord. 23 For the husband is the head of the wife as Christ is the head of the church, his body, of which he is the Savior. 24 Now as the church submits to Christ, so also wives should submit to their husbands in everything.

25 Husbands, love your wives, just as Christ loved the church and gave himself up for her 26 to make her holy, cleansing her by the washing with water through the word, 27 and to present her to himself as a radiant church, without stain or wrinkle or any other blemish, but holy and blameless. 28 In this same way, husbands ought to love their wives as their own bodies. He who loves his wife loves himself. 29 After all, no one ever hated his own body, but he feeds and cares for it, just as Christ does the church— 30 for we are members of his body. 31 "For this reason a man will leave his father and mother and be united to his wife, and the two will become one flesh." 32 This is a profound mystery—but I am talking about Christ and the church. 33 However, each one of you also must love his wife as he loves himself, and the wife must respect her husband.

6:1-9

1 Children, obey your parents in the Lord, for this is right. 2 "Honor your father and mother"—which is the first commandment with a promise— 3 "that it may go well with you and that you may enjoy long life on the earth."

4 Fathers, do not exasperate your children; instead, bring them up in the training and instruction of the Lord.

5 Slaves, obey your earthly masters with respect and fear, and with sincerity of heart, just as you would obey Christ. 6 Obey them not only to win their favor when their eye is on you, but like slaves of Christ, doing the will of God from your heart. 7 Serve wholeheartedly, as if you were serving the Lord, not men, 8 because you know that the Lord will reward everyone for whatever good he does, whether he is slave or free.

9 And masters, treat your slaves in the same way. Do not threaten them, since you know that he who is both their Master and yours is in heaven, and there is no favoritism with him.

Transformed Relationships

In Ephesians 5:21 Paul sets forth the fundamental pattern that ought to prevail among Christians: "Submit to one another out of reverence for Christ." John Calvin refers to this as "a mutual servitude" coupled with love for one another. In the following several verses Paul applies this important paradigm to three specific kinds of relationships: between husbands and wives (5:22-33), between parents and children (6:1-4), and between masters and slaves (6:5-9). In each of these sorts of relationships, care and concern for the other must take precedence over one's own interests and welfare. Duties toward the other, in line with God's will, are what's important.

In this lesson we'll discuss these relationships and how they are *transformed in Christ*.

Christian Marriage

The longer I study this exalted passage on marriage, the more the following adjectives press upon my mind: *grateful, ignorant, challenged, shamed, awestruck*. I hear the Lord speaking unmistakably to me, beckoning me—again—to undertake the steep and grand climb toward what he intends Christian marriage to be.

Grateful

Two thousand years of history have dulled the revolutionary nature of Paul's counsel here on marriage. We now take much of his teaching for granted. Back then, however, both Greeks and Jews considered women inferior. Wives had few, if any, rights. Men were allowed to divorce their wives on a whim—with a simple "bill of divorcement." Worse still, God-fearing Jews daily intoned this prayer: "Lord, I thank you that you have made me neither Gentile, nor dog, nor woman." It was a man's world back then—sadly, sinfully, indisputably.

But then the liberating good news of Jesus began to sound forth. Speaking on behalf of Christ, who died to free them and who rose from death to empower both wives and husbands to become all they're meant to be, Paul commands, "Husbands, love your wives, just as Christ loved the church . . ." (5:25).

So I'm grateful. I'm grateful to God for creating marriage in the first place (Gen. 2:18-25)—and for cleaning up spousal relationships and putting them on track after they'd become so dirty and bent by struggles over power, prestige, and worth. I'm grateful, too, for God's gracing my life with some splendid models of how marriage, at its best, can be.

Marriage is among the most remarkable gifts God has given humankind. Restored in Christ, it's a sheer wonder of grace. In some ways our modern world is still a man's world, like that ancient one that became so tired and worn out through holding women down in its vise-grip of oppression. So in the Spirit's power we all have to keep working to break down the alienation that our sin brings between men and women.

Ignorant

There are parts of Paul's teaching about marriage and about how we are to apply them today that are not fully clear to me. I am so limited in my understanding and ignorant about some of what God intends.

Paul commands, "Wives, submit to your husbands as to the Lord" (5:22). I'll freely admit that I'm not sure exactly how this injunction is to be obeyed today. The command here is not in the imperative voice in the original Greek text. Rather, it's a participle (*hypotassomenoi)* and is part of a series of participles that begins in 5:19: literally translated, these participles are "speaking . . . singing . . . psalming . . . giving thanks . . . being subject to [submitting]." Each of these, of course, is a godly thing to do and is a mark of a Spirit-filled, Christlike attitude and life. Every one of us who is in Christ, whether we're male or female, ought to be doing all of these all of the time.

Within marriage, Paul is saying, wives ought to be practicing the godly virtue of submitting themselves to their husbands—and doing so, no less, "as to the Lord" himself. Now, husbands ought never to guess that this means they may "boss" their wives around. "Bossism" of whatever sort—mental, emotional, or physical tyranny is never allowed in the husband's role.

But I'm still left with this complex question: How are husbands and wives to act in their day-to-day relationship with one another so that God's command to submit is obeyed and yet the God-given equality of both husband and wife in Christ is not violated? I've discovered that to come up with principles and theories is not too difficult, but to work them out and carry them through in practice is an entirely different matter.

Challenged

Few words in Scripture touch me more deeply or compellingly than these from Paul: "Husbands, love your wives, just as Christ loved the church . . ." (5:25). Bracing and uncompromising, this command challenges me to my very core.

Paul summons up the heady Greek word *agapao* here, and puts it in the imperative (*agapate*). It's among his favorite words to describe how we ought to act like Christ, who, though innocent of all wrongdoing, unselfishly loved his people so much that he chose the way of the cross for us.

Paul fires off five verbs to indicate the depth and breadth of Christ's love and to highlight what our Lord did for us, his church. Christ "loved" his church, "gave himself up for her" (5:25), longs "to make her holy"; and is "cleansing her" (5:26). Eventually, having completed his loving, serving work on her behalf, Christ will "present her" (5:27) as his pure and radiant bride. What a life of self-sacrificing love our Lord has shown!

Shamed

Paul's heady challenge also serves to shame me. Above my desk, facing me every day I come to work, is a little prayer by Gordon MacDonald: "Lord, above all the things you allow me to be and to do, make me a good husband and an effective father. For, by contrast, nothing else much counts."

I feel so ashamed. How often I fail to put my prayer into practice and turn these words into actual deeds of love toward my wife. Continually I must pray the medieval monk's prayer: "O Christ, who lovest me, set my own loves in order."

Awestruck

Paul says, further, that husbands "ought to love their wives as their own bodies" (5:28). "After all," husbands and wives are "one flesh" (5:29, 31; Gen. 2:24). The Greek words that Paul uses here say literally that a husband "nourishes" and "cherishes" his "body" (including his wife) "just as Christ does the church" (5:29). Reminding us here that the church is Christ's body and that we are all members of it (5:30; 1 Cor. 12:12-27), Paul is pointing out that Christ's nourishing and cherishing of the church is a *model* for the husband's relationship with his wife.

In 5:32 Paul reaches a fever-pitch of grand joy and excitement as he describes the gospel's implications for Christians who marry. He says, "This is a profound mystery—but I am talking about Christ and the church." The Greek word for "mystery" here is *mysterion,* which, translated into Latin, is *sacramentum* ("sacrament, will, testament"). The word *mysterion* itself is a sort of mystery because it's almost untranslatable. It has something of the surprising, the breath-taking, and the captivating to it. A *mysterion* is something mysterious—you could never have dreamed up the idea on your own. And because it issues from God, it inspires awe.

A Christian marriage lived out carefully and faithfully is a *mysterion,* says Paul. First, marriage itself is full of wonder, surprise, and grace. Who but God in his ever-surprising goodness and grace would have thought of creating marriage and maintaining it for us humans to enjoy? In addition, as a *mysterion,* marriage has a representational, show-and-tell quality. When a Christian couple, in imitation and honor of their Lord, day by day try to keep their vows to love each other and to submit to each other, we're inspired to say, "How like Christ this all really is! Their relationship reminds us of Christ's relationship toward his people, the church. These marriage partners really do try to forgive each other, just as God has forgiven them! And how like God they are in their faithful commitment to each other!"

Though marriage has taken some hard hits these days, God continues to call us toward something better. Our Lord's urging that we "submit to one another out of reverence for Christ" (5:21) saws against the grain of our sinful, selfish tendencies. In Christ, couples aim toward living within marriage as God intends—fruitfully, with fulfillment, and with solid joy.

Parents and Children

In Ephesians 6:1-4 Paul continues his discussion on mutual submission and honor by addressing the relationships of parents and children. Children have new duties toward their parents, and parents toward their children.

When my wife, Marcia, and I became parents, we gradually discovered that each of our children is infinitely complex; the moment we think we've got them figured out, they catch us off-guard and take us by surprise. Even under the best of circumstances—good parents, sweet children—child-rearing can be a challenge. As we've learned, there's often a great difference between how parents and children *ought to* relate and how they *do* relate.

Children are God's blessing to parents. Scripture calls children "a heritage from the LORD" (Ps. 127:3). And God calls parents to teach their children diligently (Deut. 6:6-8), for in this setting God aims to transmit his will and ways from one generation to the next. Healthy and strong families are precious and important—to parents, to their children, and ultimately to God himself.

In the Roman society of Paul's day, children were at the mercy of their father, whose *patria potestas* guaranteed him the rights to enslave them, tyrannize them, punish them mercilessly, and even sell them if he wished. William Barclay notes, "Further, the power of the Roman father extended over the child's whole life, as long as the father lived. A Roman son never came of age."

Into this sad deterioration of family relationships the gospel of Jesus burst forth with vital energy. It called for children to be good toward their fathers, obeying and honoring them, and for fathers to love their children, not exasperating or embittering them.

A child's duty toward parents is twofold: to obey (*hypakouo*), an act of submission; and to honor (*tima*), an attitude of respect (6:1-2). Further, to obey is "right" (*dikaion*, 6:1), indicating that obedience is anchored in the natural order of things.

In addition, Paul's mention of "the first commandment with a promise" (6:2) reminds us that obedience is anchored also in God's covenant with his chosen people. Any of Paul's early readers from a Jewish background would recognize the familiar words of this promise—"that it may go well with you . . ." These words often accompanied Moses' reminders that God must be obeyed (Deut. 5:16; 6:3; 6:18; 12:25, 28). What's more, Deuteronomy 12:25 adds "that it may go well with you and your children after you"; in other words, obedience brings on a chain reaction of blessing that can continue through the generations. Honoring parents—and other authority figures—will bring peace and blessing (*shalom*) to your living, as you, in turn, are honored by your children, and they by theirs. Disobedience, on the other hand, will bring trouble (a curse).

Now, if children's duty is to obey, their parents' corresponding duty is obvious: parents must be worthy of the honor they require, and they may never tire in their parental duty of insisting upon respect. Even more, parents may not exasperate their children, lest they become discouraged (see Col. 3:21). Rather, parents must encourage their children always.

How sad it is when parents take it upon themselves to berate their children. Or when a child is so coaxed and prodded by her parents' continual push to do her best that she ends up feeling tired, frustrated, humiliated, and not very worthwhile—not to them, herself, or anyone else.

Their positive duty as parents is to raise their children in the "training" (*paideia:* "discipline, healthy regimen") and "instruction" (*nouthesia:* "appropriate mindset") of the Lord (Eph. 6:4). Parents' devotion to Christ puts their relationship to their children in a new light. They become serving parents by equipping their children to be the Lord's servants.

Striking a balance between warm encouragement and sturdy discipline is hard to do, as parents know. So the wisdom and guidance of the Lord must be the foundation of all parental efforts.

Slaves/Masters (Employees/Employers)

Just as the status of women and children improved dramatically through the influence of Jesus' salvation, so did the status of slaves. Empowered by the Holy Spirit, both slaves and their masters came to see themselves as belonging to a higher master, the Lord himself. Once they acknowledged this revolutionary truth, they also began to change the way they related to one another. No longer were slaves simply chunks of protoplasm to their masters—mere "living tools," as Aristotle had classified them. (Varro, another ancient who did not believe in God, claimed he had three classes of agricultural tools: those that could speak, the slaves; those that could bellow, the cattle; and those that were mute, the implements.)

We have to admit, though, that early Christianity did not abolish the institution of slavery. Christian masters kept holding slaves, and Christian slaves, now converted and bonded to Christ, didn't (and usually couldn't) automatically free themselves from their earthly masters. Historians have noted that the ancient world in those days was so dependent on its system of slavery for trade and commerce that an abrupt end to it would have resulted in chaos. In Paul's day, out of a general population of 120 million, there were about 60 million slaves performing vital service by their manual labor.

Unlike the victims of European slave trading in the fifteenth to nineteenth centuries, these slaves were not usually people who were shipped from faraway lands but were instead mainly local people who'd been uprooted as refugees or prisoners of war, people who'd had their property seized because of Roman taxation (see also 2 Kings 4:1), or people who'd lost their freedom some other way, such as through a disagreement with ruling authorities. Convicted criminals also were part of the slave labor force.

Early Christianity did, however, bring about change that was nonetheless revolutionary. It proclaimed that both slaves and their owners now belonged to Christ, that the earthly rank of each had no final importance in heaven, and that the heart of each must be inclined with godly love toward the other. Once hearts became softened toward others in society, whomever they were and whatever their status, then society's organizations, institutions, and systems also began to change.

Today, rather than focusing on the duties of slaves and masters, we can apply Paul's instructions in Ephesians 6:5-9 to the duties of workers and their employers. The Lord calls workers, for example, to perform their tasks

- with *obedience* (*hypakouo*—6:5), doing well what the person in charge requests of them.
- with *due respect* (*phobou kai tromou*—6:5) for the authority of the person in charge.
- with a *sincere heart* (*haploteti tes kardias*—6:5)—that is, eagerly, and to the best of one's ability.
- with *loyalty* (*me kat' opthalmodoulian*—6:6)—that is, literally, "not by way of eye-service" but rather with solid devotion and earnest ambition.
- with *vital energy* (*met eunoias*—6:7)—with wholehearted eagerness and enthusiasm, as serving the Lord rather than a human being.

Employers and others in authority are to serve similarly, honoring the Lord, in whom "there is no favoritism" (6:9). While some must give orders, others must take orders; while some must lead, others must follow. Even so, Paul implies, all who are in authority must give those who serve under them proper and fitting respect. For all serve and belong to Jesus, who has authority over all (1:22; see Matt. 28:18).

One's earthly status, whether low or high, is no big deal in the Lord's final reckoning. Far more important—eternally important—is to know that one belongs to Jesus Christ. John Newton, a former slave trader whom Christ so totally set free that he never sold others again, sized up his life during his final days as follows: "My memory is nearly gone now, but two things I recall: that I am a great sinner, and that Christ is an even greater Savior."

No matter who we are, no matter what our station in life, we are all equal before God, for "all have sinned and fall short of the glory of God" and in Christ "all who believe" are made right with God (Rom. 3:22-24).

Additional Notes

5:22—In the original language, this verse contains no verb; it reads, literally, "The wives to their own husbands as to the

Lord." The verb "submit" (*hypotasso*) is actually supplied by a participle in the previous verse.

5:23—While the word for "head" (*kephale*) sometimes has the connotation of "source" or "origin," in this context it carries the meaning of "authority." The rest of the passage clarifies that this headship follows the unique, self-sacrificing example of Christ's headship for the church.

GENERAL DISCUSSION

1. How would you compare the cultural pattern for marriage in our society today (also among Christians) with the pattern that prevailed in the days of Paul? What's the same? What's different?

2. In *God's New Society* John Stott writes, "As for the wife's duty in the marriage relationship, it surprises me how unpopular this passage is among many women. When it is read at a wedding and it provokes a feminine outcry, I find myself wondering how carefully it has been read and in particular whether it has been read in its total context." How do you respond to this observation?

3. How does (or should) the guideline of mutual submission work itself out in a Christian marriage?

4. Identify a few concrete ways in which Christian parents (including yourself, if you're a parent) are often guilty of "exasperating" their children. Then identify ways in which Christian parents can raise their children "in the training and instruction of the Lord" (Eph. 6:4).

5. Read Galatians 3:28 and Colossians 3:11. If Paul said that in God's kingdom there is no more slave or free, why didn't he call for a radical break from the societal pattern of his day? What purpose could be served by asking Christian slaves to accept their slavery and submit to their masters?

6. What principles in Paul's instructions to slaves and masters can we apply to our culture's labor world today? What other biblical principles should we apply?

SMALL GROUP SESSION IDEAS

Opening (10-15 minutes)

Pray—Open your meeting with prayer, thanking God for the relationships we enjoy in society and asking the Holy Spirit to help you apply the Scriptures for this lesson to your daily living for Christ.

Share—Share how you're doing on your goals from previous lessons, and report on any group projects you may be doing.

Focus—Keep in mind the following question as you work through this lesson: *What do I value most in relationships?*

Growing (35-40 minutes)

Read (Optional)—Before moving into your discussion time, you may wish to read the Scripture for this lesson and review the comments in the study guide.

Discuss—Choose from among the following process questions as you work through the General Discussion questions.

- Have you encountered anything in Ephesians 5:21-6:9 that you hadn't noticed before? Anything that surprised you? Explain.
- What do these teachings about husbands and wives, Christ and the church, parents and children, and so on tell you about unity? In what ways can these teachings help guard believers against the world's attacks on the church?

- Reflect on a work-relationship problem in your experience (or among coworkers) that has been resolved. Which of the principles in Ephesians 6:5-9 helped to bring about resolution? What did you learn from the experience?

Goalsetting (5 minutes)
Try setting the following goal for the coming week:

- To apply what I've learned in this lesson, I'd like to commit to the following, in the strength of Christ:

Closing (10-15 minutes)
Preparing for Prayer—Share items that you'd like the others in your group to bring to God in prayer for you. Mention praises and concerns, goals you've made during this Bible study, and so on. You may also wish to read together the following statement from *Our World Belongs to God* (1986; st. 47-51):

Since God made us male and female in his image,
one sex may not look down on the other,
nor should we flaunt or exploit our sexuality.
Our roles as men and women must conform
to God's gifts and commands
as we shape our cultural patterns.
Sexuality is disordered in our fallen world;
grief and loneliness are the result;
but Christ's renewing work gives hope
for order and healing
and surrounds suffering persons
with a passionate community.

We serve Christ as singles,
whether for a time or a life,
by undivided devotion to the work of God
and so add our love and service
to the building of his kingdom.

In marriage and family,
we serve God
by reflecting his covenant love
in life-long loyalty,
and by teaching his ways,

so that children may know Jesus as their Lord
and learn to use their gifts in a life of joyful service.

In education we seek to acknowledge the Lord
by promoting schools and teaching
in which the light of his Word shines in all learning,
where students, of whatever ability,
are treated as persons who bear God's image
and have a place in his plan.

In our work, even in dull routine,
we hear the call to serve our Lord.
We must work for more than wages,
and manage for more than profit,
so that mutual respect
and the just use of goods and skills
may shape the work place,
and so that, while we earn or profit,
useful products and services may result.

Prayer—Close your meeting with prayer, asking Christ to help you live together in love for his sake, ever looking to God for guidance, ever remembering Christ's example of self-sacrificing love. Everyone may join in with prayer concerns and praises. Encourage each other to work hard at the goals you've set during this and other sessions. Before leaving, you may wish to sing together "Blest Be the Tie That Binds" or another song that focuses on unity in the body of Christ and on our care for each other in living for Jesus.

Only in God's power can we stand against the devil's schemes.

9

EPHESIANS 6:10-24

Under Attack, Standing Firm

Ephesians 6:10-24

10 Finally, be strong in the Lord and in his mighty power. 11 Put on the full armor of God so that you can take your stand against the devil's schemes. 12 For our struggle is not against flesh and blood, but against the rulers, against the authorities, against the powers of this dark world and against the spiritual forces of evil in the heavenly realms. 13 Therefore put on the full armor of God, so that when the day of evil comes, you may be able to stand your ground, and after you have done everything, to stand. 14 Stand firm then, with the belt of truth buckled around your waist, with the breastplate of righteousness in place, 15 and with your feet fitted with the readiness that comes from the gospel of peace. 16 In addition to all this, take up the shield of faith, with which you can extinguish all the flaming arrows of the evil one. 17 Take the helmet of salvation and the sword of the Spirit, which is the word of God. 18 And pray in the Spirit on all occasions with all kinds of prayers and requests. With this in mind, be alert and always keep on praying for all the saints.

19 Pray also for me, that whenever I open my mouth, words may be given me so that I will fearlessly make known the mystery of the gospel, 20 for which I am an ambassador in chains. Pray that I may declare it fearlessly, as I should.

21 Tychicus, the dear brother and faithful servant in the Lord, will tell you everything, so that you also may know how I am and what I am doing. 22 I am sending him to you for this very purpose, that you may know how we are, and that he may encourage you.

23 Peace to the brothers, and love with faith from God the Father and the Lord Jesus Christ. 24 Grace to all who love our Lord Jesus Christ with an undying love.

The Devil at Battle

Drawing this letter to a close, Paul makes clear that the world is no friend to God's people. As the Lord calls us to follow in fellowship and obedience, we can be sure Satan is lurking somewhere close by to tempt us with a counterclaim—and to fight savagely.

Satan waged heavy war against Jesus. At the beginning of his ministry Jesus was tempted by the devil for forty days (Luke 4:2), and the prince of demons kept up his attacks to the very end: while Jesus writhed in agony on the cross, willingly and obediently taking on himself the punishment for human sin, he heard Satan scream, "Come on down if you are the Son of God!" (see Matt. 27:40).

The devil raged against Jesus' earliest followers too. Take Paul, for example. Rehearsing the record of troubles he faced, Paul wrote, "Five times I received from the Jews the forty lashes minus one. Three times I was beaten with rods, once I was stoned, three times I was shipwrecked, I spent a night and a day in the open sea . . ."—on and on he goes, recalling the devil-inspired roadblocks and hardships he had to endure (2 Cor. 11:24-28).

At one point during his ministry Paul desired fervently to visit his spiritually infant friends in Thessalonica. "But," he said, "Satan stopped us" (1 Thess. 2:18). No Christian (or group of Christians) should ever expect to be handled any differently by their archenemy, the devil. Paul warned the elders of Ephesus, "I know that after I leave, savage wolves will come in among you and will not spare the flock" (Acts 20:29). And to Timothy he wrote, "Everyone who wants to live a godly life in Christ Jesus will be persecuted" (2 Tim. 3:12).

Satan's clever strategy of assault can vary widely. Paul spoke of being given a thorn in his flesh, "a messenger of Satan," to torment him (2 Cor. 12:7). But since Paul didn't go into detail, no one today knows the exact nature of the trouble. The evil one will set upon a believer with utterly devious and mischievous schemes, hoping to keep that Christ-follower from knowing and living by the promises and commands of God and from experiencing firsthand the grandeur of God's *shalom.*

Not for Wimps

The Christian life, therefore, is not for wimps. When you follow Jesus' way, be aware that you're going to be in for a fight. Again and again Scripture summons up battle metaphors to describe the circumstances we believers face. Spiritual opposition surrounds us (Phil. 1:27-30). So we must always be on guard and "fight the good fight of the faith" (1 Tim. 6:12). While at "war" with sinful influences deep within us (Rom. 7:23), we are to "stand firm" (Eph. 6:14), for the devil is "filled with fury" (Rev. 12:12). Well aware of the devil's tenacious, wily, deceiving ways, Paul encourages his readers, "Be strong in the Lord and in his mighty power" (Eph. 6:10).

Scripture's call to arms is an urgent summons never to take evil lightly but to be deliberate in resisting it. We'll never lick our wicked opponent and become victorious without being alert and intentional. Though you might wander your way into hell, you can never lolligag your way into heaven.

The wicked opponent we face is much stronger than we are. And Satan is as crafty as he is strong. "For our struggle is not against flesh and blood, but against the rulers, against the authorities, against the powers of this dark world and against the spiritual forces of evil in the heavenly realms" (6:12). Sinister and supernaturally powerful, the devil's legions oppose us all.

No amount of personal goodness we possess, no human ingenuity or savvy, however great, will ever be able to rout our spiritual enemies. We need daily, hourly, even minute-by-minute resistance. And that's possible only when we are "strong in the Lord" (6:10); our full reliance and confidence for victory must reside in no one but the God who saves and recreates us in Christ. Only in God's power can we stand against "the spiritual forces of evil." Paul calls us, then, to "put on the full armor of God" (6:11, 13). We must become skilled at putting on and using several instruments—disciplines—that can protect us spiritually and can help us resist our enemy.

"Put on the Full Armor"

Paul urges us to buckle up with "the belt of truth" (6:14). A wide leather belt was standard military issue for Roman soldiers. When tightened, it both tucked in their garments and held their swords. The belt made them combat-ready. Without it, they would trip all over themselves in their own battle dress.

Knowing how important truth is to our Christian struggle, Jesus prayed, "Sanctify them by the truth; your word is truth" (John 17:17)—and by this he meant thorough knowledge of the teachings (doctrines) of God's Word.

Are we aware of how important truth is? We live in a relativistic age in which most of our society says, "You believe your way, and I'll believe my way." Truth, our age stupidly supposes, doesn't much matter. But without equipping ourselves with the deep, enduring truths of God's Word, we'll never be fit for battle. Truth counts, and doctrine matters—a lot.

Next, we must have "the breastplate of righteousness in place" (Eph. 6:14). In spiritual battle, we need Christ's righteousness accomplished on our behalf, and in Christ's strength we are called to accomplish acts of holy and righteous living, "which God prepared in advance for us to do" (2:10). As we wrestle the evil one, we must valiantly sing into his face, "My hope is built on nothing less than Jesus' blood and righteousness." We must also do good and be holy, for weak-willed, imprudent living can drift us away from Jesus, who protects us in the fight.

Our feet must be "fitted with the readiness that comes from the gospel of peace" (6:15). Though he doesn't state it specifically, Paul is referring here to a soldier's footwear, essential gear for firm, solid footing in all situations. Christian soldiers must always be ready and eager to step forward and declare the gospel. "Always be prepared to give an answer to everyone who asks you to give the reason for the hope that you have," says the apostle Peter (1 Pet. 3:15). Indeed, "how beautiful on the mountains are the feet of those who bring good news, who proclaim peace . . ." (Isa. 52:7; Rom. 10:15).

"In addition to all this," says Paul, "take up the shield of faith, with which you can extinguish all the flaming arrows of the evil one" (Eph. 6:16). Roman soldiers carried wooden shields that measured 2 ½ feet by 4 ½ feet and were covered with metal. As the soldiers stood shoulder to shoulder, their shields formed a solid front against enemy advances. Faith does that for Christians: their trust and assurance in God unite with those of others to form a solid front against the advances of the evil one.

Also "take the helmet of salvation," urges Paul (6:17). The final defensive piece, the helmet, was designed to ward off dangerous blows to the head. Cavalry soldiers, for example, would swing mighty two-edged swords down upon foot soldiers to decapitate them. Satan's goal is to rob believers of the assurance that they belong to Christ and that their hope in him is secure.

The Christian's one offensive weapon is the "sword of the Spirit, which is the word of God" (6:17). Every Roman foot soldier carried a long, heavy knife for use in hand-to-hand combat. It's the only offensive weapon Paul mentions. Equipped with the Word of God and trained to wield it skillfully in the power of the Spirit, a Christian can win spiritual battles.

It's important to note that Paul uses the term *rhema* and not *logos* here to describe God's Word. *Logos* is a universal, all-encompassing Greek term meaning "speech, reason, discourse, word." In Greek philosophy *logos* referred primarily to the foundation of the cosmos; *logos* made the cosmos intelligible. The apostle John uses this term to refer to Jesus as the organizing center of all creation (John 1:1, 14).

The word *rhema* points to something a bit different. A *rhema* is an apt saying, an applicable word, a compelling and convincing reference. To use Scripture in combat, in *rhema*-like fashion, is to be equipped with a collection of Scriptures that apply to the combat situation at hand. Consider how Jesus, for example, used Scripture. When tempted by the evil one, he pierced Satan through by saying, "It is written: 'Man does not live on bread alone, but on every word [*rhema*] that comes from the mouth of God'" (Matt. 4:4; see also 4:7, 10).

Satan never goes away simply because we wish him to. He must be frightened into retreat. Only God's sharp, penetrating Word can do that. Confronted by God's Word, Satan will always flee—if we're skilled at using it in the Spirit's strength. In this regard we must memorize and meditate on Scripture, study it thoroughly, and apply its truths to our lives.

"And Pray . . ."

Although, strictly speaking, Paul does not include prayer as part of the Christian's spiritual weaponry and armor, he clearly underscores its vital importance here. "Pray in the Spirit on all occasions," says Paul (6:18). The Greek word for "pray" here is really a participle (*proseuchomenoi*, "praying"), which, for a specific reason, has no definite antecedent. In other words, it modifies nothing in particular—and thus it modifies everything. God is teaching us here that this entire business—outfitting ourselves with spiritual armor and then trying to use it—will fail miserably unless we immerse ourselves continually in prayer. Paul mentions a form of the word "all" four times in connection with prayer: "pray . . . on *all* occasions, with *all* kinds of prayers . . . *always* . . . for *all* the saints" (6:18). The apostle also requests prayer for himself, that he "will fearlessly make known the mystery of the gospel" (6:19).

This "mystery," again (see 3:4, 6, 9), is the too-good-to-be-true, utterly surprising nature of the good news of Jesus for all people—both Jews and Gentiles. Once we begin to realize how unbelievably good this news is, it fills us with awe and wonder. It takes our breath away.

The good news also swells us with eagerness to tell others. This is news about important, eternal matters for all people, so it's far too good to keep to ourselves, even if sharing it may bring persecution (6:19-20).

Closing Remarks

Paul closes this stirring letter with a few personal notes and a benediction. While it's important to tell the good news about eternal matters, it's also fitting to let other believers in the body of Christ "know how we are" (6:22). Sharing concerns with and caring for each other is a necessary part of being the body of Christ, united in fellowship with each other and with God. Paul notes that Tychicus, who probably delivered this letter "to the saints in Ephesus" (1:1), would give Paul's readers the necessary details on how Paul was doing—and this "dear brother" would also "encourage" them (6:21-22).

Paul adds encouragement of his own with a three-point benediction: "peace . . . love . . . [and] grace to all who love our Lord Jesus Christ with an undying love" (6:23-24). To his Gentile (as well as Jewish) readers, Paul's reminder of "grace to all" reinforces the bottom line of the gospel, which has opened the way for all believers to enjoy fellowship together and with God—the one true God who can "do immeasurably more than all we ask or imagine, according to his power that is at work within us" (3:20).

Additional Notes

6:14—"stand firm"—the notion of "standing" is clearly important to Paul because he uses it throughout his writings (see Rom. 5:2; 11:20; 1 Cor. 10:12; 15:1; 16:13; Gal. 5:1; Phil. 1:27-28; 4:1; 1 Thess. 3:8; 2 Thess. 2:15).

6:15—Believers ready themselves for spiritual battle, ironically, by embracing "the gospel of peace." Remember that the mystery now revealed is that "the Gentiles are heirs together with Israel" (3:6), and the revelation of this peace signals the defeat of the hostile powers that rule "in the heavenly realms" (3:10).

6:18—The call to pray "on all occasions"—or "at all times" (NRSV) is a familiar refrain in Paul's writings (see Rom. 1:9-10; Phil. 1:4; Col. 1:3; 4:12; 1 Thess. 5:17; 2 Thess. 1:11). The call to "be alert" reminds us of Jesus' admonition to his disciples in Gethsemane (Mark 14:38; see also 13:33-37).

GENERAL DISCUSSION

1. What does the term "spiritual warfare" mean to you? How do you experience the reality of this warfare in your life?

2. How do you respond to the following statement by Martin Lloyd-Jones? "I am certain that one of the main causes of the ill state of the church today is the fact that the devil is being forgotten. All is attributed to us; we have all become so psychological in our attitude and thinking. We are ignorant of this great objective fact, the being, the existence of the devil, the adversary, the accuser, and his 'fiery darts.'"

3. How is prayer related to the "armor of God" and the call to "stand firm"?

4. Paul began the letter of Ephesians with a wonderful rehearsal of the rich blessings believers enjoy in their relationship with Christ. Why do you think Paul closes this letter with a section on spiritual battle? What connections do you see between the beginning and end of this letter? Do you feel inspired by Ephesians 6:10-20? Why or why not?

5. Having studied the book of Ephesians, point out two or three ways in which your understanding of a benediction like the one in 6:23-24 has grown richer.

SMALL GROUP SESSION IDEAS

Opening (10-15 minutes)

Pray—Open your meeting with prayer, thanking God for protecting and caring for all of you in Christ. Also ask for the Spirit's insight as you study about spiritual warfare and look back on your study of the entire book of Ephesians.

Share—Share how you're doing on goals and group projects. During this final lesson you may also want to share with each other how your experience of doing this Bible study compares with the expectations you had as you began.

Focus—Keep in mind the following question as you work through this session: *Why is it important for me to know about spiritual warfare?*

Growing (35-40 minutes)

Read (Optional)—You may wish to read Ephesians 6:10-24 together. If you have time, you may also want to review the study guide notes before beginning your discussion.

Discuss—Choose from among the following process questions as you work through the General Discussion questions for this lesson.

- What insights have you gained about spiritual warfare in this lesson on "the armor of God"?
- Is there a piece of God's armor that you find particularly helpful in your battle with the devil? If so, what is it and why/how does it help you? Reflect on our need of "the full armor of God" in order to stand firm "against the devil's schemes" (6:11).
- Is the connection between prayer and being equipped with God's armor evident in your own life? In the life of your small group? Your church? Explain.
- What have you come across in the Scripture passage for this lesson that motivates you to live (or keep living) faithfully for Jesus? Share with your group why that's meaningful to you.

Goalsetting (5 minutes)

Try working on the following goal as you conclude this Bible study:

- Here's what I'd like to do as a result of this lesson, or, in general, as a result of studying the book of Ephesians:

Closing (10-15 minutes)

Preparing for Prayer—Share items that you'd like the others in your group to bring to God in prayer for you.

Prayer—Ask the Lord to bless you and keep you, to protect you and help you stand firm against the temptations and attacks of the evil one, and to help you apply this study of Ephesians to your daily living for Christ. Everyone can join in with personal prayer concerns and praises. In praise of who God is and all that God does for us, you might like to conclude this Bible study with a reading of Psalm 8 and a rousing song of praise and wonder to God, such as "Amazing Grace," "And Can It Be," or "Love Divine, All Loves Excelling." Encourage group members to wish each other God's strength and peace as you continue to "live a life of love, just as Christ loved us" (Eph. 5:2), serving and standing as our Lord's united body against the devil's attempts to destroy God's purposes in this world.

Group Study Project (Optional)
If anyone in your group would like to learn more about spiritual warfare, we recommend the following titles: *The Screwtape Letters* by C. S. Lewis and *Victory Over the Darkness* by Neil T. Anderson. These books are available in many Christian bookstores.

EVALUATIONS

Please fill out the evaluation form at the back of this guide. Your answers and suggestions help us as we develop other *Word Alive* studies. Thank you! Please mail evaluations to

Word Alive / Ephesians
Faith Alive Christian Resources
2850 Kalamazoo Ave. SE
Grand Rapids, MI 49560

Evaluation

Background

Size of group:

- ☐ fewer than 5 persons
- ☐ 5-10
- ☐ 10-15
- ☐ more than 15

Age of participants:

- ☐ 20-30
- ☐ 31-45
- ☐ 46-60
- ☐ 61-75 or above

Length of group sessions:

- ☐ under 60 minutes
- ☐ 60-75 minutes
- ☐ 75-90 minutes
- ☐ 90-120 minutes or more

Please check items that describe you:

- ☐ male
- ☐ female
- ☐ ordained or professional church staff person
- ☐ elder or deacon
- ☐ professional teacher
- ☐ church school or catechism teacher (three or more years' experience)
- ☐ trained small group leader

Study Guide and Group Process

Please check items that describe the material in the study guide:

- ☐ varied
- ☐ monotonous
- ☐ creative
- ☐ dull
- ☐ clear
- ☐ unclear
- ☐ interesting to participants
- ☐ uninteresting to participants
- ☐ too much
- ☐ too little
- ☐ helpful, stimulating
- ☐ not helpful or stimulating
- ☐ overly complex, long
- ☐ appropriate level of difficulty

Please check items that describe the group sessions:

- ☐ lively
- ☐ dull
- ☐ dominated by leader
- ☐ involved most participants
- ☐ relevant to lives of participants
- ☐ irrelevant to lives of participants
- ☐ worthwhile
- ☐ not worthwhile

In general I would rate this material as

- ☐ excellent
- ☐ very good
- ☐ good
- ☐ fair
- ☐ poor

Additional comments on any aspect of this Bible study:

Name (optional): ______________________________

Church: ______________________________

____

City/State/Province: ______________________________

____

Please send completed form to

Word Alive/Ephesians
Faith Alive Christian Resources
2850 Kalamazoo Ave. SE
Grand Rapids, MI 49560

Thank you!